CONTE

Leadership First

20

Must Read

Articles On

Leadership

Gifford Thomas

INTRODUCTION

The importance of leadership extends far beyond traditional management roles; it is vital in cultivating a nurturing organizational culture, uplifting team morale, and creating an environment where innovation can flourish. Effective leadership is more than just making decisions or overseeing tasks; it is about fostering trust among team members, inspiring heartfelt engagement at all levels, and demonstrating resilience when faced with challenges. Exceptional leaders strive to create spaces where everyone feels valued and empowered, allowing individuals to shine with their unique strengths and fostering a deep sense of belonging and purpose within the team.

By genuinely prioritizing the personal and professional growth of their team members and thoughtfully navigating conflicts, leaders establish a solid foundation that helps their teams excel. They champion a growth mindset, motivating individuals to embrace challenges and take meaningful risks that inspire innovation and improvement. In today's ever-changing business landscape, where unpredictability is the norm, leaders who embody adaptability and courage are essential to guiding their organizations towards success.

Moreover, leaders carry a deep responsibility: to inspire their people to reach their highest potential. This journey toward personal and collective transformation is beneficial not only for the individuals involved but also for the organization as a whole. The articles collected in this book aim to unlock this transformative potential, offering insights and strategies that can elevate individual lives and propel the organization forward in a significant way. Through this shared growth, teams can tap into their full potential, creating a lasting positive impact both within the organization and beyond.

ARTICLE 1

The Surprising Truth About Leadership: Why the Smartest Aren't Always the Greatest Leaders

A newly appointed CEO gathered with his executive team to explore strategies for the company's growth. One of his direct reports passionately outlined some ideas for increasing market share over the next five years. The CEO listened intently, but inside, he felt a wave of confusion wash over him as he struggled to grasp his manager's suggestion fully. He pondered, "Should I ask for clarification? But what if that exposes my lack of understanding and makes me seem incompetent?"

Caught in this moment of uncertainty, he recognized the challenge many leaders face: the desire to appear knowledgeable despite lacking competence in certain areas. Many individuals in leadership positions often believe that being an effective leader requires them to be the most knowledgeable and skilled person within their organization. They fear that if they don't have all the answers or expertise in every relevant area, it could signal to their staff that they are not competent or capable of fulfilling their role effectively. This perception can lead to a mentality where leaders feel they must constantly prove their intelligence and skills, which can be both stressful and isolating.

Moreover, there is a prevalent notion that an ideal leader should have a comprehensive set of skills, characteristics, and abilities to tackle any problem, challenge, or opportunity that comes their way. This view overlooks the reality that leadership is not about individual brilliance; instead, it's about fostering a collaborative environment where diverse talents and perspectives contribute to collective success.

Embracing vulnerability, seeking assistance, and valuing your team's contributions can ultimately lead to a more supportive and effective leadership approach, allowing leaders to navigate complexities with the help of their teams. This shift in perspective can alleviate some of the pressure on leaders and empower those around them to thrive and grow.

No One Is An Expert On Everything

No single person is an expert in every field; the most successful businesses thrive on collaboration among talented individuals as opposed to depending on one person. As Brian Scudamore highlights, I've learned that truly effective leaders do not seek the limelight. Instead, they focus on actively listening to their teams, promoting open communication, and fostering an environment where everyone is encouraged to share their thoughts and ideas.

Instead of trying to juggle every responsibility alone, wise leaders understand the importance of bringing together skilled professionals who shine in their areas of expertise. By creating a vibrant team of experts, leaders can confidently delegate tasks, freeing themselves to concentrate on what they do best. This approach enhances overall productivity and cultivates a team dynamic where collaboration thrives.

With the right people in key roles, a leader can step back from day-to-day operations, dedicating time and energy to essential tasks such as guiding their team, strategizing for future growth, and steering the company toward its long-term vision. This leadership style promotes innovation and strengthens the company's foundation for sustainable success.

Building A Great Team

Great leadership isn't just about knowing everything. The best leaders understand that their real power lies in creating a great atmosphere where teamwork and ongoing learning thrive. They're not afraid to admit their mistakes, showing a down-to-earth attitude and a genuine desire to grow. Instead of trying to steal the spotlight, they prioritize building a strong, united team by bringing in talented people with different perspectives and skills.

At its core, effective leadership is about lifting up those around you, harnessing everyone's smarts, and creating a shared vision that plays to each person's strengths for the good of the whole organization. This mindset shifts attention away from personal achievements to celebrating shared successes, highlighting how working together leads to fresh ideas and great outcomes.

Becoming The Most Effective Leader

Alison Griswold provides valuable insights from an interview with Lynn Good, the CEO of Duke Energy, featured in the New York Times. In this conversation, Lynn reflects on her experiences and the lessons she learned during her early tenure as CEO, particularly in the context of merging the teams from Progress Energy and Duke Energy—a significant and complex challenge.

Lynn highlights a pivotal realization she had during this transformative period: "At a certain point in your career, it's not just about being the smartest person in the room anymore." This statement underscores a crucial evolution in her leadership philosophy. As she navigated the intricacies of uniting two distinct corporate cultures and managing diverse teams, she recognized that the role of a leader extends far beyond individual intelligence or expertise.

Instead, Lynn emphasizes the necessity of evolving into the most effective leader possible by fostering the growth of those around her. She believes that true leadership involves nurturing talent, empowering employees, and providing guidance as they progress in their career paths. By focusing on developing others, she suggests that leaders can create a more cohesive, motivated, and innovative workforce, ultimately driving the organization toward greater success. Her insights remind us of the importance of collaboration and mentorship in leadership roles, especially during times of change and integration.

As a leader, one of the most insightful strategies you can adopt is surrounding yourself with exceptionally talented individuals and empowering them to shine in their respective roles. This philosophy was eloquently captured by Lee Iacocca, who famously stated, "I hire people brighter than me and get out of their way." This approach underscores the importance of recognizing that leadership is not about being the smartest person in the room; rather, it's about creating an environment where skilled team members can thrive.

Great leaders possess a profound understanding that the true engine driving a company forward is their team. Each member brings their unique strengths, perspectives, and expertise that contribute significantly to the success of the organization. These achievements stem from the unwavering passion and dedication of its employees, who not only embrace the vision of the company but also develop a deep emotional connection to its purpose. When team members are motivated and aligned with the organization's goals, they work collaboratively towards shared objectives, often resulting in innovative solutions and outstanding outcomes.

By cultivating a culture of trust and allowing individuals the autonomy to express their ideas and talents, leaders can harness the full potential of their teams. Together, with mutual respect and encouragement, you can achieve remarkable milestones that might have seemed unattainable alone. Embracing a leadership style that prioritizes the growth and recognition of your team is not just a smart strategy; it's a pathway to transforming ambitions into reality.

What Do the World's Top CEO's Have in Common? Uncovering the Key Traits

Have you ever had the incredible opportunity to work alongside a leader who truly inspires you, not just through their uplifting words but, more crucially, through their consistent actions? If you have experienced this, consider yourself among the fortunate few. Many individuals in leadership positions today lack the essential skills and qualities required to lead effectively. Consequently, a significant number of employees go to work each day merely to earn a paycheck as opposed to contributing to something meaningful or impactful.

One noteworthy example of effective leadership was VMware's CEO, Pat Gelsinger, who was recognized as Glassdoor's top CEO for 2019, boasting an impressive approval rating of 99%. This accolade offers valuable insight into the characteristics that define successful leaders. A closer examination of the most highly-rated CEOs reveals several common traits. These leaders share a deep commitment to their teams and a profound passion for making a positive difference in the world.

Through my observations, I identified seven key characteristics prevalent among these top CEOs that contributed to their ability to cultivate world-class organizations. These traits enhance employee morale and engagement while creating an environment where innovation and collaboration thrive. By understanding and adopting them, leaders can aspire to create workplaces that inspire and empower individuals to excel beyond just filling a role, enabling them to truly make a difference.

Visionary Leadership

Successful CEOs possess a clear vision for the future of their organizations. They go beyond the daily grind, looking to the horizon and planning for long-term growth and innovation. For instance, Satya Nadella, CEO of Microsoft, transformed the company by shifting its focus to cloud computing, which has grown revenue over 30% annually since its adaptation.

Visionary leaders can express their ideas in ways that motivate and inspire their teams to thrive in tough environments. For example, Howard Schultz, the former CEO of Starbucks, emphasized a vision of community and connection, helping Starbucks grow from a small coffee shop into a global brand with more than 30,000 locations. To succeed, these leaders must also be adaptable to change, ready to pivot their strategies quickly in response to shifting market demands. For instance, during the COVID-19 pandemic, many retail CEOs rushed to enhance their online services to meet the surge in e-commerce demand.

Developing People

Top CEOs prioritize the growth and well-being of both their employees and the wider communities in which they operate. They understand that success is not solely measured by profit margins but also through the impact they have on those around them. By putting the needs of others first, these leaders create an environment where their employees feel valued and empowered to reach their full potential.

In organizations that embody a strong leadership culture, every employee—regardless of whether they hold a title like "Vice President" or "Chief Executive Officer"—is encouraged to adopt a mindset and approach reflective of a leader. This inclusive philosophy fosters a sense of ownership and accountability among all team members, leading to a more cohesive and motivated workforce. What distinguishes exceptional leaders from merely good ones is their capacity to cultivate an enduring leadership culture throughout the organization. These inspirational leaders focus on continually developing themselves while actively investing their time to mentor and nurture the next generation of leaders within their ranks. By creating opportunities for professional development and encouraging innovative thinking, they build a robust network of capable leaders who can drive the organization's vision forward. This holistic approach leads to a thriving workplace, where collective success is achieved through the growth of individuals and the community as a whole.

Servant Leaders

Imagine how your business culture could change if you and your team adopted the principles of servant leadership as described by Cheryl Williamson. This approach fundamentally prioritizes the needs of others, creating an environment where both employees and customers feel valued and supported. If your organization adopted servant leadership, the impact on your customers' experiences could be profound. Imagine a workplace where leaders are not just authoritative figures who issue commands but instead, guides who empower and uplift everyone around them. Unlike traditional leaders who may adopt a more dictatorial style—barking out orders without considering the insights or needs of their team—servant leaders actively listen, engage with their employees, and create a culture of collaboration and mutual respect.

Top CEOs who embody this servant leadership philosophy invest dedicated effort into developing their staff, nurturing talents and promoting growth. They build robust cultures centered around service, emphasizing the importance of serving others as a pathway to collective success. This commitment to service extends outward, enhancing how customers perceive and interact with the business.

In a culture steeped in servant leadership, employees are more likely to feel motivated and fulfilled in their roles, leading to higher levels of productivity and engagement. As a result, customers benefit from more attentive, empathetic, and responsive service, which creates lasting relationships and builds loyalty. The ripple effects of such a transformation can elevate not just internal dynamics but also customer satisfaction and business success overall.

Effective Communication and Listening Skills

Another common trait among elite CEOs is their strong communication skills. They must convey their ideas, strategies, and goals clearly to employees, stakeholders, and customers. Take Tim Cook, CEO of Apple, as an example. His clear and transparent communication style has been a crucial factor in maintaining the loyalty and engagement of both employees and customers.

Excellent communicators foster an atmosphere of open dialogue, encouraging team members to share their thoughts and suggestions. This approach can lead to greater teamwork and a more engaged workforce. A report from Gallup revealed that organizations with highly engaged employees see a 22% boost in profitability.

Furthermore, top CEOs often excel in public speaking. They deliver presentations with confidence and clarity and understand the power of building relationships and networks. This ability strengthens collaboration and enhances influence, making it easier to achieve business goals. Top CEOs also make an unwavering commitment to listening intently to those around them. This means not merely hearing words spoken but fully understanding the underlying messages and emotions conveyed by individuals. When you give your complete attention to someone, you signal that their thoughts and feelings are valued, creating a culture of respect and open communication.

Unfortunately, many people may give the appearance of listening—nodding along or making occasional verbal acknowledgments—only to later reveal that they were not genuinely engaged in the conversation at all. This superficial form of attention can lead to misunderstandings and discontent. Active listening is more than just a useful skill; it is a vital component for anyone in leadership or management positions at any level within an organization.

The most successful CEOs excel at active listening, which involves not just passively receiving information but actively engaging with it. They seek to understand their team members' perspectives, welcome their suggestions, and appreciate their feedback. By applying active listening techniques, these leaders create an environment where everyone feels empowered to contribute, ultimately leading to a more collaborative and effective workplace.

Strong Decision-Making Abilities

Strong decision-making is essential for outstanding leadership, and this is an area where top CEOs excel. They face numerous decisions every day, from resource allocation to strategic initiatives. For example, Sundar Pichai, CEO of Google, utilizes data-driven approaches when considering the company's ambitious projects, such as the development of AI tools. His clear decisions have positioned Google as a leader in technology.

Successful CEOs combine data analysis with intuition for informed decision-making. They scan the landscape, weigh their options, and anticipate potential outcomes. By balancing logical thinking and a drive for innovation, they can effectively navigate challenges and seize opportunities. These leaders also have the courage to take calculated risks. They embrace the idea that failure can be part of the journey to success and are willing to learn and adapt. A study found that 70% of successful CEOs have experienced significant failure in their careers, yet they used those experiences as learning opportunities.

Lifelong Learning Commitment

For many top CEOs, the journey to success doesn't stop once they reach the top. Lifelong learning is a common theme among the best in business. Industry leaders must keep track of trends, tech advancements, and changing customer preferences. For example, Mary Barra, CEO of General Motors, has emphasized the importance of staying informed, particularly as the automotive industry rapidly shifts towards electric vehicles.

CEOs often engage in personal development through formal education, mentorship, or self-motivated learning. They understand that being knowledgeable and adaptable is critical in a constantly evolving business landscape. Research shows that organizations emphasizing learning opportunities experience a 50% increase in employee retention. Moreover, this emphasis on learning creates a growth culture within their organizations. By encouraging teams to pursue skills and knowledge, effective leaders foster innovation and resilience.

Genuinely Caring For Their People

According to Cheryl Williamson, a leader who genuinely demonstrates care and concern for their team is unlikely to face issues with loyalty or subpar customer service. These leaders prioritize the well-being of their employees above purely financial considerations. When a leader invests time and effort into nurturing their team, they create an environment where employees feel valued and supported, which in turn drives them to provide exceptional service to customers.

There are numerous ways to express appreciation and care for your team members creatively. For instance, a simple gesture such as presenting a $5 gift card to their favorite store can brighten someone's day and show that you recognize their individual preferences. Additionally, being mindful and offering compassionate words of support during difficult personal times can foster a sense of trust and connection.

Whether it's facilitating team-building activities, providing flexible work hours, or just checking in regularly to ask how they're doing, these small actions cumulatively make a significant impact on team morale and performance. Ultimately, when employees feel genuinely cared for, they are more likely to go above and beyond in their roles, leading to satisfied and loyal customers.

Top CEOs are dedicated to a service-oriented approach, prioritizing the needs of their employees and stakeholders above their own interests. This selfless leadership not only fosters a positive organizational culture but also contributes to remarkable employee satisfaction; these exceptional leaders often enjoy approval ratings exceeding 90% among their workforce.

Consider this: if you were to conduct a survey of your employees, what would your approval rating be? How would they assess your leadership? This self-reflection can provide invaluable insights into your effectiveness as a leader and the overall morale within your organization. Understanding these key traits can provide valuable insights for aspiring leaders. By emulating these traits, individuals can develop strong leadership skills and confidently navigate their careers. As the business world continues to change, embracing these traits may be the ticket to becoming a successful leader in any field.

ARTICLE 3

Leaders Who Create Fear-Based Organizations Are Doom To Fail, Here's Why

David made a significant decision to leave his job, which became toxic and demoralizing. Despite his dedication and hard work, he found himself increasingly disillusioned as he witnessed a disturbing trend: the most talented and innovative employees were the ones who chose to resign, while those who engaged in sycophantic behavior were the ones steadily climbing the corporate ladder into management roles. It was a culture that stifled creativity and discouraged initiative; ideas were often dismissed or ignored, leaving the visionary thinkers feeling marginalized and frustrated.

The tipping point for David arrived when a completely unqualified individual with a personal connection to one of the company's vice presidents was elevated to be his manager. This person lacked the skills necessary to lead effectively, but their relationship with upper management overshadowed any qualifications. It was beyond frustrating for David to witness this blatant favoritism, and it ultimately pushed him to the brink. After much contemplation, he made the difficult choice to resign from a job for which he had poured so much passion and effort into building his career.

As he walked out of the office for the last time, he felt an overwhelming sense of relief, as if a heavy burden had been lifted from his shoulders. The oppressive atmosphere that had been weighing him down was finally behind him. I came across this story in an article by Liz Ryan in Forbes, and it resonated deeply with me. It reflects the experiences of countless individuals in organizations around the world.

It serves as a poignant reminder of how great employees who enter the workplace with an inspired heart and bright ideas aimed at making a difference can quickly become uninspired and demotivated. They soon realize that the environment does not foster growth or innovation but instead inhibits their potential and stifles their enthusiasm for their work.

Fear Base Management

It's truly remarkable how prevalent the phenomenon is where individuals in management and leadership roles resort to instilling a culture of fear as a means to motivate their teams. This approach baffles me, especially considering the extensive research demonstrating that fear-based leadership is fundamentally ineffective. While it might yield short-term compliance or productivity, the reality is that the overall quality of work tends to be merely average, and the results are rarely sustainable over time.

Liz Ryan offers an insightful perspective on this issue by pointing out what lies at the heart of a fearful manager's psyche. Contrary to what one might expect, their primary fear isn't necessarily the potential for business failure. Instead, their greatest concern revolves around the possibility of someone in their vicinity challenging their authority or competence. This fear often stems from a fragile ego, which drives them to prioritize their self-image over the well-being of their team and the organization.

In many cases, this ego appears to overshadow even the fear of the business collapsing, leading to a toxic work environment that stifles innovation and employee engagement. Ultimately, this cycle of fear hampers individual performance and can adversely impact the organization's overall success in the long run.

Some People Are Just Not Ready To Lead

Promotion within organizations often hinges on an individual's performance in their current role, as highlighted by Jim Harter, Gallup's Chief Scientist. This practice typically leads to the promotion of high achievers—those who excel in sales, accounting, or other specialized fields—into managerial positions after demonstrating expertise and longevity in their roles. However, this approach to career advancement can present significant challenges.

Research indicates that the skills and talents contributing to an employee's success in their previous non-management roles seldom align with those required for effective management and leadership. Many new managers find themselves in positions of authority without the necessary training or skillsets to excel in their new roles. Alarmingly, Ken Blanchard has pointed out that nearly 47% of organizations lack formal training programs for new supervisors. This gap often leaves newly promoted managers ill-equipped to lead their teams effectively.

The consequences of promoting individuals into management without proper training can be quite detrimental. Organizations may end up with numerous ineffective bosses rather than inspiring leaders. According to Liz's insights, less competent individuals can sometimes rise to prominent positions within fear-based organizational cultures.

This occurs because these individuals pose little threat to current leadership; in toxic environments, being non-threatening often emerges as a primary job requirement. Such dynamics can foster a culture where mediocre talent thrives, ultimately limiting the organization's growth and effectiveness.

Pseudo – Leader

It is crucial to exercise discernment when evaluating individuals who claim to assume the role of a leader, particularly those displaying what can be described as Pseudo-Leadership tendencies. Often, these individuals exhibit a self-serving mentality, prioritizing their own interests and welfare over the well-being of their teams and organizations.

This self-centered approach not only jeopardizes the integrity of the leadership but also cultivates a culture of fear among employees. Many workers, especially those who have spent considerable time in such environments, become accustomed to a toxic workplace culture. They may start to believe, erroneously, that this type of management style and company culture is standard across the business world.

As a result, these employees often find themselves trapped in a cycle of fear and anxiety, leading them to accept behaviors that would otherwise be considered unacceptable. For instance, it may become routine for them to witness their managers engaging in gossip about colleagues or to endure the humiliation of being yelled at in front of others.

This state of constant fear can have profound implications for employee morale and productivity. Many employees develop coping mechanisms that include avoiding interactions with their managers, even going so far as to hide when they realize they've made a mistake or need assistance.

This behavior underscores the severe psychological toll that such a toxic work environment can impose. According to Liz, a knowledgeable observer of workplace dynamics, those engulfed in such environments often struggle to recognize the extent of their fear and the detrimental impact it has on their mental health while they are still within that context. However, when individuals finally escape from these oppressive circumstances, they often gain a stark clarity about the toxicity they endured.

They come to realize how significantly the management style and attitudes of their leaders contributed to fostering an environment rife with discomfort and anxiety. Such revelations can be eye-opening, highlighting the essential role leaders play in shaping a positive or negative workplace culture. Fear has no role in management and leadership; in fact, it is entirely counterproductive.

When leaders resort to fear to motivate their team, they undermine the very essence of effective leadership. Tom Flick emphasizes that employing fear as a strategy disempowers employees, redirecting their focus inward rather than outward toward the organization's goals. Employees operating under a climate of fear tend to enter a survival mode, prioritizing job security over the broader needs of the company. This mindset shift inhibits their ability to engage with their roles fully, which means they become less concerned about the company's overall success, the quality of the products or services they provide, or their customers' experiences. Instead, their primary focus becomes navigating the workplace landscape cautiously to avoid conflict or repercussions.

According to Rose Krivich, the repercussions of fear-based management extend beyond individual employees—they can create a ripple effect that negatively impacts employee engagement, customer satisfaction, and even brand reputation. When employees are engulfed in stress and apprehension, these feelings often manifest in their interactions with clients. A fearful workforce can lead to unsatisfactory customer experiences and, ultimately, tarnished organizational credibility.

Moreover, discontent stemming from a toxic workplace culture can propagate beyond the immediate environment. Employees may voice their frustrations through word of mouth or on social media platforms, which serves as a cautionary signal to potential candidates considering employment with the organization. This negative feedback loop can significantly hinder recruitment efforts, as the perception of a fear-driven culture can deter top talent from seeking opportunities within. It is crucial to recognize the importance of a healthy workplace atmosphere; never accept a toxic, fear-based organization as the norm. Environments steeped in fear are detrimental not only to professional growth but also to personal well-being and energy levels. Fortunately, there are many alternative workplaces that prioritize positive engagement and support. Embrace these opportunities because you deserve a fulfilling, respectful, and empowering work environment.

ARTICLE 4

Mental Health: The Silent Struggle of Leaders and How to Safeguard It

For a long time, mental health has often been perceived as a concern primarily affecting others, leaving many individuals to distance themselves from the possibility that they, too, could face such challenges. Conditions like depression and anxiety seemed remote and foreign to those who considered themselves to be "normal" or unaffected. However, as the demands of our increasingly fast-paced and high-pressure world grow, it has become evident that mental health struggles can impact anyone, regardless of their status or achievements.

A tragic illustration of this reality is the untimely death of renowned fashion designer Kate Spade. At the age of 55, she was found in her New York City apartment, the victim of an apparent suicide. This shocking loss underscored how even those who project an image of success and happiness can be grappling with profound inner turmoil. Despite her remarkable accomplishments in the fashion industry and her ability to create a brand that resonated with millions, Kate battled depression for years—a fight she chose to face largely in silence, away from the public eye.

Her story is a sobering reminder of the critical importance of recognizing mental health as a vital aspect of overall well-being. It serves as a call to action for society to cultivate an environment where individuals feel safe to express their struggles and seek support. The need for compassion, understanding, and open conversations about mental health has never been more urgent as we strive to support one another through the complexities of life.

A recent study indicated that a staggering 64% of senior business leaders report having faced mental health challenges, including anxiety, stress, and depression. This alarming statistic prompts a deeper examination of the factors contributing to these struggles, particularly the intense pressures associated with leadership roles. The demands of overseeing teams, making critical decisions, and navigating often unpredictable business landscapes can create a high-stress environment.

Many individuals ascend to leadership positions based on their technical skills and expertise but find themselves lacking the necessary training and support to effectively manage the emotional and psychological complexities of leading others. This can lead to overwhelming feelings of isolation and burnout as they grapple with the burdens of responsibility without the right tools to cope.

The consequences of this lack of preparation extend beyond the individual leaders. Their mental health struggles can ripple through the organization, affecting team dynamics, employee morale, and overall productivity. A leader's state of mind significantly influences the workplace atmosphere, and if they are struggling, it can create an environment of stress and uncertainty for their teams.

Therefore, creating a compassionate workplace culture that prioritizes mental health is essential. Organizations should implement initiatives that provide mental health resources, promote open conversations about psychological well-being, and offer training programs that equip leaders with the skills to manage their own mental health. By taking these steps, companies can enhance the well-being of their leaders but also create a more supportive and resilient working environment for everyone. The pressures that often accompany demanding jobs, like frequent travel and time away from loved ones, can really take a toll. It's concerning to see the stigma that surrounds mental health, especially when it's linked to leadership capabilities.

We must approach this issue with empathy and create an open dialogue about how workplace stress can affect mental well-being. It's essential that we challenge the misconceptions surrounding mental health and leadership while prioritizing the availability of diverse support services for those in senior positions. Everyone deserves compassion and assistance in navigating these challenges.

Emotional Intelligence

Higher levels of emotional intelligence (EI) play a crucial role in reducing individual stress and enhancing the overall effectiveness of teams within organizations. Emotional intelligence encompasses a range of skills, including the ability to recognize and manage one's own emotions, as well as the capacity to identify and respond appropriately to the emotional distress experienced by others. This dual capacity is vital for fostering a collaborative and supportive workplace environment. A significant study conducted among top executives at 15 prominent global companies, such as Pepsi, Volvo, and

IBM, highlighted the critical importance of emotional intelligence in leadership.

The findings, as reported by the Chartered Management Institute, suggested that the key to success at the upper echelons of these organizations is largely attributable to emotional intelligence rather than merely technical or intellectual competence. This insight reinforces the idea that effective leadership requires more than just industry knowledge or skills; it necessitates an understanding of human emotions and interpersonal dynamics.

Moreover, developing emotional intelligence involves cultivating self-awareness, which is the ability to recognize and understand one's emotions and their impact on behavior. This self-awareness allows leaders to reflect on how their feelings influence their decisions and interactions with others. By gaining a deeper understanding of their emotional landscape, leaders can better navigate challenges, make informed choices, and respond constructively to the needs and concerns of their teams.

Learn To Manage Your Stress

In today's fast-paced and often overwhelming world, stress has become a prevalent issue for many individuals. The relentless pace of daily life, combined with numerous responsibilities and pressures, can lead to increased feelings of anxiety and even depression. When these negative emotions escalate, they can have a profound impact on both our personal relationships and our professional endeavors.

During an interview, the late Susan Wojcicki, former CEO of YouTube, recently shared her insights on this critical issue, emphasizing the importance of taking time off to reflect and re-energize. This perspective highlights a simple yet effective strategy for managing stress and mental health: the necessity of stepping back and allowing oneself a moment of respite.

In practice, carving out time to retreat into a quiet and comfortable space can produce significant benefits. This solitude provides an opportunity for reflection, helping individuals to reconnect with their inner thoughts and feelings. By engaging in self-reflection, we can gain clarity about our priorities and assess what truly matters to us.

Furthermore, focusing on the aspects of your work that are within your control can substantially alleviate the emotional weight we often bear. When we redirect our attention towards manageable tasks and set achievable objectives, the sense of empowerment can counteract feelings of helplessness and stress.

Ultimately, it is vital to prioritize self-care during challenging times. Recognizing and addressing our mental health needs is essential for not only overcoming obstacles but also for fostering personal and professional growth. By taking proactive steps to care for ourselves, we lay the groundwork for resilience, allowing us to navigate life's complexities with greater ease and confidence.

Educate Yourself

It is crucial to educate ourselves about the signs of stress and anxiety, as emphasized by expert Nicola Brown. Recognizing the early warning signs that someone may be feeling overwhelmed or in conflict can significantly enhance our workplace culture and well-being. Early signs of stress may include changes in behavior, mood swings, decreased productivity, withdrawal from social interactions, or even physical symptoms like fatigue and headaches. By remaining vigilant and observant, we can identify when a colleague might be in distress. If you observe someone struggling or exhibiting these signs, consider extending a gesture of kindness and understanding.

Reaching out to a colleague can be as simple as asking how they are doing or if they would like to talk. Suggesting a break to recharge, whether it's a short walk, a coffee break, or a moment of mindfulness, can provide them with an opportunity to step away from their stressors. Additionally, offering to facilitate a supportive conversation—either with you or a member of the HR team—can create a safe space for them to express their feelings.

Listening with empathy and compassion is essential in these moments; it assures your colleague that their experiences and emotions are valid. Providing an open ear and a non-judgmental atmosphere can help them feel valued, understood, and less isolated in their struggles. Remember, creating a culture of mental wellness benefits everyone and can lead to a more resilient and productive workplace overall.

Re-energize Yourself

Finding a secondary passion can be an excellent way to create balance in our lives, as noted by Graham Jones. Take rower Alison Mowbray, for instance—despite the intensity of her athletic training, she always made time for the piano. This commitment not only led her to win a silver medal at the Olympics in 2004 but also nourished her love for music, making her an accomplished pianist, too.

Similarly, many successful businesspeople find joy in their hobbies; Richard Branson is well-known for his adventurous spirit in hot-air ballooning. Even simple activities like playing bridge or attending the opera can provide a meaningful escape for busy executives, helping them to recharge and refocus. These moments of joy are essential for our well-being.

Depression is a common struggle that many people face, and it is absolutely treatable. It's important to remember that experiencing mental health challenges does not reflect any lack of character. Unfortunately, stigma around mental health persists in our society, affecting us all. As someone who has faced depression and anxiety, I feel a strong responsibility to bring attention to this issue.

Leadership can be incredibly demanding, and research indicates that those in top positions often grapple with various challenges, including narcissism, over-optimism, fear, anger, and, yes, depression. You don't have to navigate this journey alone. As Nicola Brown points out, it can be daunting to admit when we're feeling overwhelmed, but reaching out for support is a brave and essential step.

Talk to a trusted friend or loved one—building a support system is crucial. Finding the strength to lift yourself out of a depressive state requires immense courage, and it's vital to remind yourself that you are here, you matter, and it's important to let go of the stress over things beyond your control. Embrace each day with hope—release your worries and allow yourself to live fully and authentically.

ARTICLE 5

Great Leaders Create An Environment That Allow Their People To Be Themselves, You Should Too.

In my book, The Inspirational Leader: Inspire Your Team to Believe in the Impossible, I recount a deeply impactful story shared by Chelene Pedro that illustrates the critical importance of communication in leadership. The narrative centers around a CEO who faced significant challenges in his interactions with one of his managers.

During a tense meeting, a minor issue unexpectedly escalated when the CEO raised his voice over a seemingly trivial matter. Although the subject was minor, the CEO's angry outburst reverberated down the corridor, creating a palpable sense of discomfort among the staff, who were left to witness this breakdown of professional decorum. The atmosphere in the office shifted dramatically, underscoring how rapidly tensions can escalate in a work environment, especially when leaders fail to communicate with respect and clarity.

The manager, understandably rattled by the CEO's reaction, made the difficult decision to leave the office. Moments later, he returned with a handwritten resignation letter, which he had promptly dated "effective immediately." This poignant choice highlighted not only his dissatisfaction but also served as a powerful reminder of the weight our words and actions carry. This story serves as a crucial lesson for leaders, emphasizing that the way we communicate—especially under stress—can profoundly impact team morale and cohesion. In leadership, fostering an environment of respect and understanding is essential for inspiring teams to believe in their capabilities and potential.

Many leaders outwardly demonstrate a genuine concern for the success of their teams and express a strong commitment to fostering an environment where individuals can thrive. They seem dedicated not only to helping their members achieve organizational goals but also to empowering them to reach their full potential in various aspects of life, including personal and professional growth. At first glance, these leaders appear to embody the essential qualities of true and inspirational figures, evoking respect and admiration from their teams.

However, as time progresses, certain underlying qualities of these leaders can begin to emerge, revealing complexities that may impact their effectiveness. In some instances, individuals in leadership roles may, whether by design or as a result of unawareness, cultivate an environment that proves challenging for their team members. This can manifest as micromanagement, lack of transparency, or ineffective communication, which collectively create a workplace atmosphere that feels toxic.

In such environments, employees may find themselves shifting their focus toward self-preservation rather than collaboration. Rather than working together to strengthen the organization and innovate, team members might spend their time seeking new job opportunities or developing exit strategies to escape the discomfort of their current situation. This tendency can lead to increased stress and disengagement, deeply affecting both individual well-being and the overall health of the workplace.

It is crucial to recognize the profound impact your leadership styles and behaviors can have on the morale, productivity, and mental health of employees. A supportive and empowering leadership approach can enhance job satisfaction and foster a sense of belonging, while a toxic leadership environment can quickly undermine these efforts, making it essential for leaders to self-reflect and seek continuous improvement in their leadership practices. A leader plays a vital role in shaping the environment that ultimately defines the culture within a company. This culture has a profound influence on employees' productivity and their level of engagement.

For instance, in a supportive and understanding workplace, individuals feel empowered to acknowledge their mistakes or request assistance, expressing sentiments like, "I made a mistake" or "I need some help." According to Simon Sinek, this reflects a leader who has successfully cultivated an atmosphere where team members feel safe to be authentic and vulnerable without fear of judgment or repercussions.

On the other hand, when the workplace atmosphere creates a sense of insecurity, employees may find themselves more focused on self-preservation. This can manifest in behaviors such as sending "cover your ass" (CYA) emails after every meeting or conversation, driven by the fear of being blamed or facing negative consequences.

This reaction signals that the leader has inadvertently created a toxic culture where individuals feel isolated and competitive rather than collaborative. In such environments, it seems as though every person is left to navigate the challenges alone, resulting in a sense of mistrust and disengagement.

It's crucial for leaders to recognize these underlying dynamics within their teams. By promoting open dialogue and encouraging a culture of support and acceptance, they can cultivate a workplace where everyone feels valued, understood, and motivated to contribute. Ultimately, a compassionate and proactive leadership approach can transform the workplace into a thriving community, benefiting both the individuals and the organization as a whole.

Life can often present us with an array of challenges that can feel overwhelming. In these times, it becomes crucial, particularly for those in leadership roles, to take a step back and reflect on how we can support and uplift those facing difficulties. It's remarkable how a simple act of kindness—a warm smile exchanged in passing or a few comforting words during a tough moment, can have a profound effect on someone who is struggling. These small gestures, often seen as trivial, can become beacons of hope for individuals whose lives may feel chaotic or turned upside down. Effective leadership is fundamentally anchored in compassion and the ability to provide support. It goes beyond merely guiding a team to achieving organizational goals; it is about building an environment where individuals feel empowered to express their true selves and pursue their fullest potential. Exceptional leaders create spaces that not only encourage creativity and collaboration but also promote emotional well-being, ensuring that everyone feels valued and understood.

When leaders prioritize the development of their team members, they ignite a sense of purpose and collective unity centered around a shared vision. This vision acts as a unifying force, inspiring each team member to contribute their unique strengths toward a common goal. Great leaders recognize that their success is intricately tied to the achievements of those they lead; thus, they reject the notion of personal glory in favor of a service-oriented mentality. By uplifting those around them, these leaders reaffirm the overarching mission and purpose of their organizations. They remind everyone involved that they are working together toward a bigger picture, creating a sense of belonging and community. This approach not only strengthens individual bonds but also enhances overall team dynamics, empowering everyone to navigate challenges together with resilience and hope. Through this commitment to uplifting others, leaders create a culture where everyone can thrive, ultimately benefiting the organization as a whole.

ARTICLE 6

The Power Of Appreciation

Do you value your team? Do you value the people you work with? Do you value people on the whole?

I recall one night when I worked tirelessly with a team from 11 p.m. to 6 a.m. to repair a ruptured water line at a facility. The intensity of the work was overwhelming, especially under the harsh conditions and with a smaller team than usual. Despite the challenges we faced, we remained focused on getting the job done.

When we finally completed the task at 6 am, I couldn't help but reflect on what truly stood out that night. It wasn't the lengthy hours or the freezing weather that impacted me; no, it was the feeling of being unappreciated by the project manager. Recognition and support can make a significant difference, especially in challenging situations like what we encountered that night. I remember when one of the team members asked the manager if he could arrange breakfast for everyone.

The manager responded, "We are paying you guys to do the job and walked off," with no acknowledgment of the hard work the guys put in or any expressions of gratitude. Reflecting on it now, I realize that some individuals believe that compensation alone is sufficient and that appreciation isn't necessary. This reminds me of how important it is to recognize and value each other's efforts, as a simple thank you can go a long way in creating a positive work environment. It's a bit disappointing to see leaders still holding onto outdated mindsets. If they embrace change, their organizations can truly thrive in today's ever-evolving world.

If leaders approach their role without genuine appreciation for their team, they risk missing out on the incredible potential that lies within their members. In the 21st century, it's crucial for leaders to connect with and value their people authentically. As John Maxwell wisely points out, the most essential quality of a leader is their capacity to cherish and uplift others.

Without this, an organization may struggle to thrive and, unfortunately, remain average. Valuing people is at the heart of creating a thriving team. Nurturing a culture of appreciation can truly transform how we work together. When employees feel genuinely valued, their engagement and motivation soar, allowing them to be their best selves.

A leader that recognizes and honors each individual's contributions not only enhances performance but also cultivates a warm, supportive, and inclusive environment. Understanding the profound impact of appreciation fosters trust and deepens relationships, leading to a culture where team members wholeheartedly celebrate one another's efforts. This, in turn, creates an uplifting atmosphere that significantly boosts morale and collaboration.

A recent Gallup study sheds light on the amazing benefits of appreciation in the workplace! It shows that employees who receive regular recognition and praise actually perform 14% better than those who don't—how incredible is that? It's essential to remember that showing appreciation doesn't always have to be formal; even those little, everyday acts of gratitude can truly brighten a team's day.

Just taking a moment to share a genuine "thank you" during your daily interactions can really uplift someone's spirits in ways we might not even realize! As a leader, it's essential to never take your team for granted. Make it a priority to appreciate your people and acknowledge their commitment genuinely. Valuing their contributions and thanking them for their efforts creates a positive environment and reinforces their sense of belonging and motivation. Remember, your recognition can be a powerful source of inspiration and encouragement for your team. When people feel genuinely appreciated, they tend to go above and beyond what is expected of them.

Taking a moment to express our genuine gratitude not only uplifts everyone on your team but also encourages a culture of appreciation that inspires everyone to give their best.

ARTICLE 7

The Psychological Benefits Of Feeling Valued

When I started my first job right after school, I struggled with my self-esteem. This uncertainty made me hesitant to take on new challenges. I ended up creating stories in my head to justify the limits I placed on myself. I can still recall my supervisor noticing my lack of confidence; it was pretty clear to him. He kindly said, "You have so much potential! Just remember that if you don't believe in yourself, you might hold yourself back." His words stuck with me!

His words lingered in my mind, and at that same time, I had the wonderful opportunity to hear the late Dr. Myles Munroe speak, and he shared some truly powerful insights about our unique gifts. Dr. Munroe emphasized that when we embrace our special talents and share them with the world, we have the incredible potential to become extraordinary. His words really resonated with me and inspired a shift in my mindset. I began to speak positively to myself, saying, "Gifford, you can do this; you've got the ability to achieve your goals and dreams!"

Gradually, I began to embrace this newly acquired perspective, and over time, my life underwent transformations that I had not previously deemed possible. The individual who once grappled with a deficiency of confidence started to thrive; I moved from self-doubt to self-belief, and this underscores the psychological advantages of feeling valued.

Feeling valued is not just a nice idea; it is a vital aspect of our mental and emotional well-being. When you value yourself, and people add to that value by recognizing your worth, you experience several positive psychological effects. Feeling valued comes from recognition, respect, positive feedback from others, and, most importantly, yourself. This sentiment is closely linked to fundamental human needs, such as belonging, self-esteem, and happiness. Research indicates that people who feel valued are more motivated and productive.

A University of Minnesota study found that employees who received recognition for their efforts were 14% more productive than those who did not. This acknowledgment prompts a sense of happiness and satisfaction, fostering a willingness to engage deeply in various activities. One of the most significant psychological benefits of feeling valued is its link to self-esteem. Self-esteem is all about how we see our own worth, and it's so important for our personal growth and happiness. When we feel valued, it boosts our self-worth and helps establish a strong, positive self-image. When individuals receive recognition at work for their efforts, it truly helps them believe in their own abilities.

As leaders, it's important for us to recognize that this kind of belief fosters confidence and encourages a growth mindset, which is essential for continuous personal development. By celebrating achievements—like reaching sales milestones or successfully completing a project—your team members often experience an incredible boost in their self-esteem.

Additionally, feeling valued significantly impacts the relationships people form with those around them. When individuals feel appreciated, they are more likely to reciprocate, resulting in healthier and more meaningful interactions. This cycle of mutual appreciation creates an inviting atmosphere where individuals feel respected and secure. Research in the Journal of Personality and Social Psychology found that relationships marked by appreciation and respect lead to a 45% increase in overall satisfaction. Such strong bonds contribute to emotional health, providing a sense of belonging that acts as a buffer against the stresses of life. Another critical benefit of feeling valued is its effect on emotional resilience—the ability to bounce back from challenges. When individuals experience appreciation, they are often better prepared to face adversity. Feeling valued serves as a psychological buffer against life's difficulties.

For instance, a study showed that individuals who received regular expressions of appreciation reported a 28% increase in their ability to deal with stress effectively. This sense of security empowers individuals to chase their goals confidently, leading to improved well-being. The psychology of feeling valued also contributes to developing a positive mindset. Positive psychology emphasizes the importance of nurturing experiences that promote well-being. People tend to concentrate on their strengths and achievements when they feel appreciated. This positive focus encourages a growth-oriented attitude, helping individuals embrace challenges and learn from their experiences.

Individuals who feel valued are 30% more likely to exhibit a positive outlook, contributing to greater overall life satisfaction. Feeling valued can show up in many environments, such as homes, schools, or workplace communities. The essential principle remains the same in each context: acknowledgment fosters a sense of worth. In family settings, expressing appreciation strengthens bonds and creates supportive environments. For instance, families that regularly celebrate each other's milestones notice a 20% improvement in family cohesion. In schools, recognizing students for their efforts can lead to a 25% boost in academic performance and a more positive school climate.

A strong sense of community can significantly enhance the feeling of being valued. When individuals feel appreciated by their community, it strengthens their connection and boosts their self-worth. Being recognized by a group fosters a sense of collective identity and purpose. Communities marked by appreciation often exhibit higher levels of trust, cooperation, and empathy. Studies show that such environments can lead to a 50% increase in community members' overall happiness.

The psychological benefits of appreciation are evident; as a leader, this is one of your most powerful strategies for inspiring and motivating people to become the very best version of themselves. Now, let's examine how leaders can create a culture of appreciation. We will also explore some case studies that highlight the significance of appreciation and how it helped transform an organization's culture, leading to increased profitability.

ARTICLE 8

Creating A Culture of Appreciation.

Ken Blanchard, co-author of The One Minute Manager, said, "If there is one thing I've learned in my life, it is the fact that everyone wants to be appreciated." Adopting a culture of appreciation in the workplace is not just about creating goodwill; it is a strategic decision that can reshape how employees interact and work. The benefits, from improved engagement to reduced turnover, highlight the vast impact that recognition can have on an organization.

In today's world, taking even a moment to express appreciation can lead to meaningful changes in workplace dynamics. Embedding appreciation into your organization will boost morale and create a more productive, innovative, and cohesive work environment. Implementing an appreciation culture requires a dedicated commitment to valuing each team member's contributions. This investment will pay off by creating a brighter future for your organization and a more satisfying work experience for everyone involved.

Employee appreciation is significant for various reasons. It is a fundamental cornerstone of organizational culture and reflects essential aspects of human psychology. Recognizing and validating an individual's efforts, skills, and contributions in the workplace is crucial for ensuring that employees feel valued. A strong culture of gratitude flourishes through the active involvement and dedication of all individuals within the organization, from executive leadership to management and employees alike.

Leaders play a crucial role in ensuring that a culture of appreciation is successful. Remember, leaders establish the tone for others to follow; therefore, they must demonstrate effective communication through both their words and actions to embed this culture into the very fabric of the organization. According to Inspirus, the following are best practices and recommendations for cultivating a positive workplace culture that recognizes the distinct strengths of each employee.

1. **Provide frequent opportunities for thankfulness:** Build moments of gratitude into team meetings and regular communication.

2. **Recognize and reward behaviors, not just achievements:** Don't wait for a big win to acknowledge the efforts of the team

3. **Personalize your shows of appreciation**: Different employees have different preferences on how they like to be acknowledged – some thrive in the spotlight, whereas others prefer more private affirmations.

4. **Always be authentic:** Meaningful appreciation has to feel genuine to both the giver and the receiver. Be specific **in your praise.**

5. **Provide a platform and digital tools:** Make it easy for managers and peers to express their gratitude to each other.

The most extraordinary workplace cultures truly excel when they effectively integrate recognition and appreciation, cultivating an environment where employees feel genuinely valued for their individual contributions. **Recognition** involves acknowledging an employee's achievements, big or small and publicly celebrating their efforts and successes. This practice reinforces positive behaviors and motivates others to strive for excellence.

On the other hand, **appreciation** goes deeper,

focusing on the inherent worth of each individual and the unique skills they bring to the team. It's about expressing gratitude for the daily contributions employees make— recognizing their hard work, dedication, and the passion they invest in their roles.

When these two elements—recognition and appreciation—are harmoniously intertwined, they create a supportive and uplifting atmosphere. This culture leads to increased job satisfaction, enhanced teamwork, and higher employee retention rates. Employees feel more engaged and inspired to innovate and collaborate, knowing their efforts are seen, valued, and celebrated. Ultimately, this synergy not only enhances individual morale but also contributes significantly to the overall success and cohesion of the organization.

In Barbara Mitchell and Cornelia Gamlem book The Big Book of HR, they shared how The Ritz-Carlton Hotel Company uses recognition to inspire and retain their staff. According to Mitchell and Gamlem, The Ritz-Calton has demonstrated that employee recognition significantly contributes to retention rates.

It maintains the lowest employee turnover rate among hotel chains and asserts that the recognition of employees is a crucial factor behind its elevated retention rates. High retention rates positively impact financial performance. "With engaged employees, I can drive our revenue per available room 20-30 percent higher than if I have employees who come in and just do their jobs," says Kathleen O. Smith, senior vice president of human resources at the company's headquarters in Chevy Chase, Maryland.

When Sheldon Yellen was Belfor Holdings CEO, he wrote approximately 12,000 Handwritten Birthday Cards, anniversary cards, thank you notes and messages to his staff to show his appreciation for their outstanding work. When asked why do it, why write all these birthday cards when your assistant or someone in the company can quickly produce these cards for you. Yellen Responded

"Maintaining that handwritten note as a practice, as a habit, I think is important because it really differentiates you from these e-mails and texts that go on; it lets people know and understand that they matter. I get to drop a little note in each birthday wish, and they feel remembered and valued."

So when Yellen turned 60, he got an appropriate gift—more than 8,000 handwritten birthday cards from BELFOR employees, who wanted to show their appreciation for the CEO's tradition. According to Yellen, "One of the cheapest things you can do in life, to make a difference, is just being nice." "That's what we should all be striving to do every day because random acts of kindness are invaluable to the people we serve every day. Now, let us examine the advantages of instituting a culture of appreciation in greater detail.

Enhances Employee Engagement

When employees feel valued and appreciated, their dedication to the organization grows even stronger. This sense of engagement not only lifts their enthusiasm but also sparks greater productivity. Studies reveal that companies with robust employee recognition programs see engagement jump by over **14%**, leading to improved job performance and lower turnover rates.

Engaged employees are more likely to go the extra mile—they share innovative ideas and enthusiastically take part in projects, which boosts the company's chances of achieving its goals. In fact, organizations that score high on engagement can enjoy an impressive **18% increase in productivity**!

Build a Positive Work Environment

Fostering a culture of appreciation truly helps to create a warm and positive work atmosphere where everyone feels valued and recognized. When team members take a moment to acknowledge each other's efforts, it builds not just camaraderie, but also a strong sense of mutual respect.

In these supportive environments, employees are much less likely to feel disheartened by the challenges they face. Instead, they find motivation in a network that celebrates every success, big or small! Research shows that teams that embrace positive recognition practices enjoy a remarkable 25% lower turnover, especially during stressful times.

Builds Stronger Team Relationships

Regularly recognizing each other's efforts really boosts

team spirit! When everyone feels appreciated, it helps build trust and deepens connections among colleagues. This improved communication fosters a fun and collaborative atmosphere that can truly enhance how well the group works together. For example, companies that promote recognition among peers often witness a fantastic 30% jump in teamwork efficiency. This stronger collaboration creates a vibrant environment where everyone feels more at ease sharing their ideas.

Drives Improved Performance

Recognition plays a significant role in boosting performance! When employees feel that their hard work truly matters and will be appreciated, they're inspired to strive for excellence. This passion can enhance the quality of their work and foster a sense of ownership over the results. Leaders can make the most of this by linking appreciation with specific performance achievements.

For instance, when an employee exceeds a sales target, giving a shout-out for that success can motivate them to reach even greater heights. Organizations that weave recognition into their performance data often enjoy an impressive 10-15% boost in overall performance!

Reduces Employee Turnover

When we emphasize appreciation, it really helps keep our talented team members on board. Employees tend to stick around longer in workplaces where they genuinely feel recognized and valued. In fact, research shows that when employees feel appreciated by their employer, they're 60% more likely to remain loyal to the company over time. This not only lowers turnover rates but also saves companies on recruitment expenses and creates a positive environment enriched by the insights and experiences of long-standing employees who truly understand the company's values and culture.

As leaders, when we genuinely integrate the power of appreciation into our strategic approaches, we cultivate a workplace environment that thrives on inspiration and motivation. By recognizing and valuing the contributions of each team member, we foster a culture where individuals feel seen and valued. This, in turn, ignites their passion for their work and encourages a sense of ownership and commitment to our collective goals. When appreciation becomes a cornerstone of our leadership style, it not only enhances team morale but also promotes collaboration and innovation, leading to a more engaged and productive workforce. In essence, a consistent practice of appreciation transforms our workplace into a dynamic hub of creativity and enthusiasm, ultimately driving the success of our organization.

ARTICLE 9

Uncovering The Untapped Potential: Fostering Kindness In Leadership

In today's hectic work environments, the definition of effective leadership is constantly evolving. Among the emerging traits, kindness stands out as vital, having the power to reshape workplaces and fuel success. But what does it truly mean to encourage kindness in leadership? Let's explore the importance of kindness in leadership and how it leads to better performance, stronger relationships, and a healthier workplace culture.

The Essence of Kindness

Kindness in leadership is more than just being nice; it involves empathy, understanding, and a sincere concern for the happiness of others. Leaders who show kindness nurture an environment where team members feel valued and appreciated.

Research shows that workplaces with high kindness scores see a **70% increase in employee morale**, which translates to higher engagement and productivity. When kindness is a priority, it builds trust—an essential component for effective teamwork. Teams with high levels of trust experience **25% higher performance** because employees feel comfortable sharing ideas and taking creative risks.

Additionally, kindness creates a supportive atmosphere. Collaboration flourishes in teams led by kind leaders. A report from the Harvard Business Review indicates that employees in compassionate workplaces are **50% more likely to share their ideas** freely. This nurturing spirit enhances creativity and innovation, allowing teams to tackle projects with enthusiasm. Moreover, leaders who exhibit kindness can lower stress levels within their teams. This reduction in stress contributes to a more sustainable and enjoyable work experience, with employees reporting decreased burnout by approximately **60%**.

THE BENEFITS OF KIND LEADERSHIP

Enhanced Employee Engagement

Leading with kindness leads to heightened employee engagement. When team members feel acknowledged and respected, their motivation skyrockets. Statistics reveal that engaged employees are **21% more productive** than their disengaged counterparts. This commitment fosters a sense of ownership over their work, contributing to not only individual performance but also team loyalty.

Improved Communication

Kindness opens up lines of communication. Leaders who approach conversations with empathy create an environment where team members feel safe sharing their thoughts and concerns. This openness boosts collaboration and assists in resolving conflicts, increasing overall team cohesion. In fact, companies that prioritize kind communication experience a **30% reduction in misunderstandings and disputes**.

Greater Resilience

A culture of kindness strengthens team resilience. During challenging times, leaders who show kindness offer the support needed for team members to overcome hurdles. This emotional encouragement fosters strong bonds between team members, which is critical for navigating difficulties. Studies have shown that teams with higher empathy levels are **40% more resilient** when faced with adversity.

One of the simplest ways to promote kindness is to lead by example. Leaders should consistently demonstrate kindness in their interactions. Phrases like "thank you" or actively listening to a colleague can set the tone for kindness in the team's culture. Moreover, encouraging team members to perform acts of kindness can cultivate a friendly work atmosphere. Simple initiatives like a "kindness board" can allow employees to recognize each other's efforts, creating a positive feedback loop. Additionally, team-building activities that focus on supportive interactions can help build relationships based on kindness.

As leaders, it is imperative to invest in training centered on emotional intelligence and interpersonal skills. This training can significantly improve communication effectiveness and provide actionable strategies to enhance daily interactions within the team. However, if there is no feedback mechanism in place to measure how kindness is being implemented and practiced in your organization, all of the above will be a wasted effort.

Regularly seeking feedback from team members can highlight how kindness manifests in the organization. This input can identify areas for improvement while showcasing instances where kindness positively impacts team dynamics.

Another way to measure kindness in leadership is by integrating it into performance metrics. Leaders can evaluate their effectiveness not only based on results but also on how they treat team members and foster a kind atmosphere. This approach encourages leaders to consider their interpersonal behaviors as seriously as their operational goals.

Creating a culture of kindness in leadership is an investment that yields numerous benefits, including higher employee engagement, improved communication, and increased resilience. The value of kindness in leadership is immense, providing a foundation for a thriving and productive environment. By implementing practical strategies and committing to lead with kindness, leaders can unlock potential within their teams and create a positive workplace culture that drives growth and success.

ARTICLE 10

The Challenge Of Leading In A Culture Of Distrust

Jim sat down with his manager for a performance review over the past six months, and he was taken aback by the feedback he received. His manager said,

"Jim, you need to be tougher with your team. Show them who's in charge."

The organization had developed quite a toxic culture, but Jim had always prided himself on being a positive exception. It was disheartening for him to feel pressured to adopt a management style that contradicted his personal values and leadership approach. As time went on and the pressure became increasingly overwhelming, Jim ultimately made the difficult decision to leave the company. His team was stunned and saddened by his departure.

It's hard to blame Jim; how can anyone inspire and lead effectively in an environment filled with distrust between employees and management? One of the most common challenges leaders face, as highlighted by David Horsager, is the misconception that trust comes automatically with their title. It's important to recognize that trust is not something that is bestowed upon you because of your position.

It must be nurtured and earned, which can take significant time and effort. Building trust is a journey that requires patience, dedication, and a deep sense of integrity. It's not something that can be easily fabricated or achieved through shortcuts. Trust is much like a forest; while it can take years to flourish, it can be lost in an instant due to carelessness. Acknowledging this can lead to more meaningful connections with those we lead.

Creating a positive workplace environment is crucial for ensuring that employees feel welcomed, valued, and excited about their work each day. Ideally, employees should anticipate coming to their jobs, finding fulfillment not only in the tasks they perform but also in overcoming challenges, building meaningful relationships with their colleagues, and experiencing an overall uplifting atmosphere.

As marketing expert Neil Patel highlights, the nature of work can occasionally be demanding and stressful. However, it is essential that the culture within the workplace serves as a buffer against this stress rather than adding to it. A positive workplace culture should provide a sense of security, encouragement, and camaraderie that allows employees to thrive. To foster such a compassionate culture, organizations can implement various strategies, such as promoting open communication, recognizing and celebrating employee achievements, encouraging teamwork and collaboration, and providing opportunities for professional development. These initiatives can significantly enhance employees' experiences, making them feel more engaged and motivated.

Ultimately, a workplace that prioritizes a supportive and nurturing culture creates an environment where employees not only perform at their best but also genuinely enjoy their time at work. This sense of belonging and positivity can lead to improved morale, increased productivity, and reduced turnover, benefiting both the employees and the organization as a whole.

As a leader, you may possess the authority to direct and influence others within your organization or team. However, the effectiveness of your leadership extends far beyond mere positional power. Without cultivating a strong and trustworthy character, it can be extremely challenging to genuinely guide and inspire those around you. Inspirational leadership is rooted in the ability to maintain a steady and reliable presence, especially during times of uncertainty or change.

It's imperative that your character remains steadfast and does not fluctuate with every external circumstance. Over time, individuals within your team will develop a keen sense of your true intentions and motivations. They will assess whether you embody the qualities of a genuine leader or if you merely don the facade of authority. This process of evaluation is gradual and intuitive; people are naturally attuned to the authenticity of those who lead them.

Striving to cultivate authenticity in your leadership approach is paramount. When you demonstrate consistency in your values and actions, you foster an environment of trust, which in turn motivates others to engage meaningfully with you and the mission at hand. Authentic leadership encourages open communication, collaboration, and mutual respect, all of which are essential for creating a more supportive and cohesive team dynamic. Ultimately, this dedication to integrity and authenticity not only enhances the overall effectiveness of your leadership but also leads to a more engaged and motivated team eager to contribute to shared goals.

Every job comes with its own set of challenges, as Lisa Tyan points out—even on the best days. However, if the mere thought of going to work leaves you feeling exhausted, downhearted, or even physically unwell, it might be more than just typical job stress; these can be signs of a toxic work environment.

Work should never feel like a sentence to endure, waiting for the moment you can finally leave at 4 or 5 PM. Given how much time we spend at work, it should ideally feel like a supportive extension of our home life. I truly believe that every organization has the potential to be a wonderful place to work.

A toxic workplace isn't born from a few negative individuals but often stems from leadership that either fails to recognize or chooses to overlook the signs of an unhealthy environment. As Shahnaz Broucek, a professor of coaching and mentoring at the University of Michigan, notes, "Leadership sets the tone of the workplace culture and acceptable behavior patterns."

Ultimately, it's the responsibility of leadership to identify the root causes of team dysfunction and work toward solutions. But what happens if the leader is part of the problem? Hmm, great question; this means the leader must get it right with themselves first before they can get it right with their team.

ARTICLE 11

How To Shift From Doing The Job To Inspiring Others

Leadership is frequently perceived as a sequence of responsibilities encompassing direction, oversight, and execution. However, a notable transformation occurs upon fully embracing a leadership position: one transition from merely performing tasks to inspiring your team to become the very best version of themselves. This adjustment not only alters one's personal perspective but also significantly impacts the engagement, creativity, and performance of the team. Let's explore strategies that leaders can employ to cultivate an inspiring environment that motivates their teams to excel.

Understanding the Leadership Shift

When you focus on achieving goals, it's easy to get caught up in details and day-to-day tasks. A hands-on approach may yield quick results, but it can also limit long-term growth for you and your team. As leaders, your role shifts to creating a vision, recognizing potential, and building an empowering culture.

This requires moving from being a doer to becoming a motivator. To become an inspiring leader, start by understanding what drives each team member. Engage in one-on-one conversations to learn about their aspirations, challenges, and passions. For instance, if a team member aspires to develop a new skill, help them connect with training resources or mentorship opportunities. Tailoring your leadership approach to meet individual needs builds a stronger, more engaged team.

Crafting a Vision

A clear vision serves as a guiding roadmap for your team, steering them toward a shared goal. When you express your vision with clarity and passion, it inspires your team to align their efforts accordingly. Use storytelling to make your vision relatable and compelling. For instance, when launching a new project, share a story about how it can positively impact both the team and the community.

This approach not only engages imagination but also instills a sense of resilience and determination. Your team must recognize that their contributions are part of a larger narrative. A 2022 study found that 87% of employees are more engaged when they understand how their work contributes to a broader company vision. This sense of purpose transforms routine tasks into meaningful actions, boosting motivation and performance.

Embracing Authenticity

Authenticity in leadership is essential for building trust. Being open about your values and experiences allows your team to feel safe expressing themselves and taking risks. Demonstrate vulnerability by admitting mistakes and sharing lessons learned. If a project you led didn't turn out as expected, discuss what went wrong and how you would approach it differently next time.

This honest dialogue encourages others to learn and grow, building mutual respect and open communication. Such genuine interactions create an environment where individuals feel inspired to be their best selves.

Encouraging Innovation

Leadership involves nurturing a culture of innovation. Challenge your team to think creatively and question the status quo. Encourage brainstorming sessions where everyone feels free to share their ideas without fear of criticism. When innovation flourishes, it paves the way for unexpected solutions and growth opportunities.

Consider implementing an "innovation hour" each week, allowing team members to explore new ideas or approaches. Recognize and celebrate contributions, whether big or small. By valuing diverse perspectives, you create a culture of collaboration where everyone is actively engaged. Fostering an innovative mindset enhances problem-solving skills and drives overall success success.

Empowering Others

Empowerment is a vital aspect of inspiring leadership. Give your team the tools, resources, and authority they need to take ownership of their work. For example, allow team members to make decisions about their projects rather than directing every detail. When team members feel empowered, they commit more to their roles and engage deeply in their tasks.

Instead of micromanaging, focus on providing constructive feedback that promotes growth. A 2023 survey found that 70% of employees reported increased job satisfaction when they felt empowered in their roles. Empowering your team creates a ripple effect, boosting their confidence and encouraging them to inspire others in their roles.

Building a Supportive Culture

A supportive culture is the backbone of inspiring leadership. Creating an environment where team members feel comfortable sharing ideas and challenges. Being approachable and attentive reinforces this culture. Implement practices that encourage team building and recognition. Acknowledge individual and group achievements regularly, no matter how small.

Studies show that recognizing employees increases engagement by up to 80%. Such acknowledgment not only boosts morale but also inspires further efforts. By creating a culture of support, you uplift individuals and build a strong team dynamic that can achieve remarkable results.

Maintaining Your Own Inspiration

Inspiring others is truly a two-way street! To be an effective source of inspiration, it's essential to nurture your own passion and stay connected to the reasons that sparked your desire to lead in the first place. Embrace opportunities for continuous learning and personal growth, whether that's through attending workshops, diving into insightful books, or seeking out a mentor.

Studies show that leaders who make learning a priority can boost team innovation by an impressive 61%! When you demonstrate a commitment to growth, it naturally encourages others to strive for improvement as well. Equally important is finding that balance between work and self-care. Make your well-being a priority; it's vital for staying mentally and physically fit. When leaders take care of themselves, it beautifully inspires their teams to adopt similar habits for their health and growth.

Transitioning from merely doing tasks to inspiring others is a rewarding journey, filled with challenges and opportunities. Recognizing that your role as a leader is rooted in inspiration rather than execution leads to significant rewards. By crafting an engaging vision, embracing authenticity, encouraging innovation, empowering your team, building a supportive culture, and nurturing your own inspiration, you can transform your leadership approach.

As a leader, your responsibility lies in creating a space where team members can thrive. Remember, when you inspire others, you unlock their potential, and together, you can achieve extraordinary things.

ARTICLE 12

How Teamwork Transforms Organizations

In today's fast-paced work environment, teamwork is vital for success. It extends beyond merely working together; it encourages collaboration, increases productivity, ignites innovation, and boosts employee morale. In the tech world, only a few icons have shone as brightly as the late Steve Jobs, the co-founder of Apple Inc. Jobs and his team transformed the tech industry by revolutionizing the way we interact with technology daily.

While many credit Jobs' creativity with Apple's success, he often highlighted the crucial role of teamwork. As he famously said, "Great things in business are never done by one person. They are done by a team of people." Recognizing the incredible power of teamwork and its impact on any organization's success.

The Role of Teamwork in Organizational Success

Teamwork is all about people coming together to achieve a shared goal. When we collaborate, each team member can share their unique strengths, perspectives, and skills to create something truly amazing. For example, research from Google shows that teams that work closely together see a 30% boost in performance compared to those who don't emphasize teamwork. Plus, organizations that value teamwork enjoy much better communication. When team members participate in open discussions, they gain a deeper understanding of each other's roles, which fosters trust and helps eliminate barriers, leading to a more cohesive work environment.

Teamwork also plays a crucial role in how satisfied employees feel. According to Gallup, companies with engaged teams enjoy 21% higher profitability. When team members feel supported and connected, they're more likely to stay committed, which helps lower turnover rates and creates a more stable organization.

And let's not forget the beauty of diversity in teamwork! In today's globalized world, teams often consist of individuals from varied backgrounds, and this diversity is a true treasure, bringing a broader range of ideas and solutions to the table.

For instance, research from McKinsey reveals that organizations ranking in the top quartile for racial and ethnic diversity can outperform those in the bottom quartile by a remarkable 35% in financial performance. To fully embrace this diversity, it's essential for companies to foster an inclusive culture where every voice is genuinely appreciated.

By encouraging open communication and ensuring psychological safety, all team members can share their ideas freely and confidently. In such a nurturing environment, innovation flourishes, paving the way for fresh insights and creative solutions. Moreover, diverse teams connect more effectively with their customers, addressing their varied needs and enhancing customer satisfaction satisfaction.

Building Trust and Effective Communication

Trust is truly the heart of effective teamwork! When trust is present, collaboration thrives, making all the difference. To nurture this vital trust, organizations can establish clear communication expectations. Regular check-ins and constructive feedback go a long way in building strong connections.

Utilizing collaborative tools like project management software is also key! Tools such as Trello or Asana allow team members to share information easily, boosting collaboration and efficiency. Moreover, embracing healthy conflict can really elevate team dynamics. By facilitating respectful discussions about varied opinions, teams can make even better decisions. In fact, a study from the Harvard Business Review shows that teams encouraging constructive conflict are five times more likely to reach high performance

Nurturing a Positive Team Culture

Building a positive team culture is essential for unlocking the full benefits of teamwork. Companies should create spaces where everyone's effort is recognized, achievements are joyfully celebrated, and meaningful connections are nurtured. Engaging in team-building activities, recognition programs, or even casual get-togethers can really spark personal interactions among colleagues.

Additionally, investing in professional development strengthens team bonds and shows employees they're valued. In fact, studies from LinkedIn reveal that companies focusing on employee learning enjoy 60% lower turnover rates. By promoting growth, organizations demonstrate a real commitment to collaboration and building a vibrant culture of continuous learning. When team members feel appreciated, they're more likely to share their ideas and get involved actively. This collaborative spirit not only creates a lively work environment but also drives the organization toward its goals and objectives.

Measuring the Impact of Teamwork

To truly understand the impact of teamwork, organizations should actively measure it. This can be achieved through employee surveys, performance assessments, and tracking outcomes. Regularly evaluating the effectiveness of teamwork helps identify areas for improvement and strategies that work.

Analyzing metrics such as project completion rates and employee engagement can reveal the connection between teamwork and performance. A Gallup survey shows that companies with highly engaged teams experience 17% higher productivity. By demonstrating how teamwork drives company success, leaders can strengthen support for collaboration initiatives.

As a leader, your ability to create amazing teams is truly the heart of your organization's success. With the right tools and a nurturing teamwork culture, companies can engage with a variety of talented individuals, igniting even more innovation and creativity.

It's essential for organizations to actively support teamwork. Emphasizing continuous improvement and learning from experiences empowers teams to adapt to changing needs. Ultimately, a strong commitment to teamwork can reshape not just the organization but its entire industry. The real potential lies within each team, just waiting to be discovered!

ARTICLE 13

Fearless Leaders: A Person Who Never Made a Mistake Never Tried Anything New

Great leaders are often romanticized as a journey filled with inspiration and success. However, many of these leaders throughout history have faced numerous challenges, setbacks, and failures. The famous quote, "A person who never made a mistake never tried anything new," captures the essence of courage and creativity.

Many people see the perks of leadership, but many leaders pay the price of leadership as well. When you are striving to become one of the greats, you will stumble; you will have to learn from your mistakes and evolve to ensure you are growing with the pace of change. The most successful leaders have often encountered criticism or been labeled as failures. What sets them apart is their commitment to embracing mistakes as part of the creative process.

Take Thomas Edison, for example. When he worked on developing the lightbulb, he famously stated, "I have not failed. I've just found 10,000 ways that won't work." This perspective doesn't just highlight resilience; it shows how learning from failure allows for continued refinement until success is achieved. By viewing each misstep as a chance to grow, leaders can adapt and improve their ideas.

Fear can often be a big hurdle for many of us, and it's surprising how it can even freeze talented individuals in their tracks, making it tough to take the necessary risks. Yet, some of the greatest engineers, artists, and dreamers have discovered a way to turn that fear into motivation rather than letting it hold them back. Just think about J.K.

Rowling, the brilliant mind behind the Harry Potter series. Before she found incredible success, she faced numerous rejections from publishers—over a dozen, as a matter of fact! Instead of succumbing to despair, Rowling decided to polish her manuscript and keep going. That steadfast determination not only established her as a household name but also transformed modern literature for young readers everywhere globe.

Great leaders challenge the status quo and motivate individuals to explore uncharted territories. They consistently embrace new opportunities, even at the risk of making mistakes. In the tech industry, many startups begin with numerous pivots and adjustments. For instance, Elon Musk encountered significant challenges with SpaceX in its early years, including failed rocket launches.

Nonetheless, his unwavering curiosity about space travel fueled groundbreaking innovations that transformed the aerospace sector. Musk famously stated, "If things are not failing, you are not innovating enough," highlighting that embracing failure is essential for success.

Learning from Failure: Case Studies of Resilient Leaders

1. Steve Jobs and the NeXT Computer

After being ousted from Apple, Steve Jobs founded NeXT, a computer platform development company. Initially, NeXT struggled to gain traction in a competitive market. However, the lessons learned during its difficult early years taught Jobs about user-friendly design and experience. Eventually, when Apple acquired NeXT for approximately $429 million, Jobs returned to lead Apple into a new era with revolutionary products like the iMac, which saw sales increase by 40% over the previous year.

2. Oprah Winfrey and Her Early Career

Oprah Winfrey's journey was fraught with setbacks, including being fired from her early job as a news anchor. However, rather than letting this moment define her, Oprah shifted her focus. She developed a talk show that eventually became a global phenomenon, drawing in around 10 million viewers per episode at its peak. Her resilience in the face of adversity showcases the power of perseverance and adaptation in finding one's true calling.

3. Walt Disney and His Bankruptcy

Walt Disney faced several challenges, including the bankruptcy of Laugh-O-Gram Studios, his first animation company. Instead of letting this setback derail him, he continued to create, ultimately founding The

Walt Disney Company, which became a multi-billion-dollar global brand. His story reinforces how embracing failure can lead to extraordinary success when combined with passion and hard work.

Organizations that encourage risk-taking and view mistakes as learning opportunities often cultivate environments where groundbreaking ideas flourish. Leaders play a crucial role in this process by creating an atmosphere of open communication where team members feel safe to share their thoughts. Recognition and appreciation of those who take risks—regardless of the outcome—help build a culture of innovation.

Practical Tips for Embracing Mistakes

1. **Shift Your Perspective**: Treat mistakes as opportunities for learning. This mindset can lead to new ideas and solutions.

2. **Encourage Team Collaboration**: Create an environment that values collaboration. Sharing

experiences will help everyone learn from each other's journeys.

3. **Set Small Goals**: When trying something new, break the process into manageable tasks to ease the fear that accompanies larger risks.

4. **Reflect and Grow**: Analyze what went wrong and how to improve in the future. Reflection is vital for personal and team growth.

5. **Celebrate Small Wins**: Recognize every achievement, big or small. This approach encourages risk-taking and fosters a positive mindset towards innovation.

The quote, "A person who never made a mistake never tried anything new," beautifully captures the essence of true leadership. The inspiring stories of fearless leaders remind us that mistakes are just a natural part of our journey.

Often, the road to success is lined with missteps, but it's through these challenges that remarkable leaders emerge. Embracing our mistakes not only fosters personal growth but also encourages future generations to boldly venture toward a brighter future. So, the next time you face a setback, keep in mind that it could be a stepping-stone to something truly extraordinary!

ARTICLE 14

The Hidden Costs Of Tolerating Toxic Employee Behavior

In today's fast-paced job market, the success of any organization hinges on productivity and employee morale. However, the presence of toxic employees often goes unnoticed until it's too late. Tolerating negative behaviors can have severe consequences, leading to diminished productivity, increased stress, and higher turnover rates. Understanding and addressing toxic behaviors is essential for leaders who wish to create a positive workplace culture.

Understanding Toxic Behavior

Toxic behavior can take many forms, such as chronic negativity, passive-aggressiveness, and outright hostility. These behaviors can create a harmful work environment that affects not only the individuals exhibiting them but also their colleagues and the organization as a whole.

Toxic behaviors often arise from deeper personal issues, such as job dissatisfaction or misalignment with company values. A study by the Harvard Business Review indicates that approximately 70% of employees reported experiencing toxicity at work due to unresolved conflicts. Recognizing these underlying causes is vital for addressing toxic behaviors effectively. When these toxic behaviors go unchecked, team dynamics can suffer tremendously. A toxic employee can erode trust and collaboration, resulting in resentment and divisions among team members.

Research shows that one toxic employee can negatively impact the morale of up to 12 other colleagues. In any organization today, teamwork is essential, and as a result, this can lead to missed deadlines and compromised quality of the company's products or services. For example, teams plagued by toxicity can see a decline in innovative thinking.

A positive work atmosphere fosters creativity; however, negativity stifles it. This is evident as companies with engaged employees reported 21% higher profitability, highlighting the connection between a healthy work environment and business success.

A spin-off of this is employee turnover, which is one of the most significant costs associated with allowing toxic behavior to persist. When toxicity is rampant, engaged employees may leave in search of healthier environments, resulting in a loss of valuable talent. The cost of replacing an employee can reach as high as 150% of their annual salary when considering recruiting, hiring, and training expenses.

Additionally, the departure of experienced employees can disrupt team cohesion and lead to a loss of institutional knowledge. To illustrate, if a team of 10 experienced workers leaves due to a toxic colleague, the organization could incur losses of up to $1 million when factoring in the costs of hiring replacements and decreased productivity during the transition period.

Decreased Productivity and Performance

Another hidden cost of tolerating toxic behaviors is a gradual decline in overall productivity. When employees are surrounded by negativity and conflict, their focus diverts from work tasks to emotional turmoil. Studies reveal that employees experiencing high levels of engagement are 17% more productive than their disengaged counterparts A toxic environment, conversely, can lead to disengagement, resulting in reduced output and lower quality of work.

For instance, a project team may take 30% longer to complete tasks if team members are preoccupied with unresolved conflicts or avoidance of a toxic colleague. As these delays accumulate, they can severely impact project deadlines and client satisfaction. Trust, respect, and collaboration form the backbone of a healthy workplace culture. However, tolerating toxic behaviors can strain these elements.

Employees may begin to withdraw, creating an atmosphere rife with fear, mistrust, and hostility. Diminished relationships can stunt collaboration, stifling the organization's growth. A detrimental workplace culture not only affects current employee engagement but can tarnish reputations and hinder efforts to attract new talent. Organizations must prioritize open communication and establish clear behavior expectations to maintain a positive culture. Encouraging feedback and promoting teamwork can help build a supportive community focused on shared goals.

Addressing toxic behavior is about much more than simply removing negative influences; it is about creating a workplace where all employees can succeed. Leaders need to establish clear boundaries and expectations for acceptable behavior and provide the necessary support for employees who may need help. Employees should feel safe and comfortable discussing concerns related to toxic behaviors, whether regarding their teams or interpersonal relationships.

Offering training and resources can also be beneficial for both leaders and staff in recognizing and addressing toxic behaviors. Providing resources such as employee counseling or conflict resolution programs can promote a healthier work environment. Lastly, implementing a zero-tolerance policy for any toxic behavior communicates that such actions are unacceptable.

This clear stance can significantly build a healthier workplace. Allowing toxic employee behavior to persist can result in hidden costs that undermine an organization's culture, productivity, and overall success. Swiftly recognizing and tackling these behaviors is crucial to maintaining a positive workplace.

By providing a safe space for open communication, establishing clear expectations, and offering necessary support, organizations can effectively combat toxicity and create an environment conducive to growth and collaboration. Investing in a healthy workplace culture is not just beneficial; it is essential for long-term success.

ARTICLE 15

The True Essence Of Leadership: The Power Of Empowering Others

Leadership is often misinterpreted as directing and controlling people and processes. However, a closer look reveals that the true essence of leadership lies in empowering others. It is not about occupying a top position; rather, it is about cultivating an environment where individuals feel confident and capable of taking initiative.

Empowerment can transform not just teams but entire organizations. Understanding this fundamental aspect of leadership helps us build more collaborative, innovative, and resilient workplaces.

Understanding Empowerment

Empowerment involves enabling individuals to make decisions, take ownership, and work independently. It means providing people with the authority, resources, and opportunities they need to succeed in their roles. This does not mean offering a lack of direction; instead, it includes setting clear goals while also offering support and guidance. When leaders promote empowerment, they create a culture where employees feel trusted and valued, resulting in higher morale and productivity. For example, companies implementing empowerment strategies report a 20% increase in employee satisfaction.

The Myth of Authority

Many leaders mistakenly equate authority with effective leadership. However, relying solely on authority can create a culture of fear and compliance. Employees may follow orders but often without enthusiasm, which can suppress creativity and initiative. Instead of focusing on power, leaders should prioritize building relationships based on trust and respect.

A study found that teams with empowered members contribute 30% more innovative solutions. When individuals feel empowered, they are more likely to take risks, share ideas, and actively contribute to the team's success. **Engagement increases** because employees feel that their contributions are meaningful. This engagement boosts job satisfaction and retention rates, with companies experiencing up to a 25% reduction in employee turnover. When your team can think freely, they are more inclined to suggest creative solutions. Empowered individuals are not afraid to challenge the status quo, leading to advancements and improvements. However, to genuinely empower others, leaders need to implement strategies that actively promote this mindset.

Here are specific steps leaders can take:

1. Encourage Open Communication

Create a safe space where team members can freely share their thoughts and ideas. Actively seeking feedback shows you value their input. One effective method is holding monthly team meetings to facilitate open dialogue.

2. Delegate Responsibilities

Trust your team with responsibilities that align with their strengths. For instance, if a team member excels in data analysis, assign them a significant project related to analyzing performance metrics. This trust not only boosts their confidence but also helps them develop their skills.

3. Provide Resources and Support

Ensure your team has access to the tools and training they require to succeed. For example, provide subscriptions to online courses or access to project management software, enabling them to perform their roles effectively.

4. Recognize and Celebrate Achievements

Acknowledging both individual and team successes reinforces their importance. Regular recognition can lead to a 30% increase in morale, motivating team members to maintain their commitment.

5. Foster a Growth Mindset

Encourage your team to embrace learning and development. Normalize discussing failures as learning opportunities instead of setbacks. This approach allows team members to experiment and enhances creativity within the team.

While the idea of empowerment is appealing, applying it can be challenging. It requires patience and a willingness to adapt. Start with small changes, such as delegating less critical tasks at first and gradually increasing complexity as team members grow more confident. But most importantly, model the empowered behavior you wish to see.

Make decisions collaboratively and demonstrate adaptability in your leadership style. By showing trust and a willingness to relinquish control, you inspire your team to do the same. Several leadership styles prioritize empowerment, making them effective in promoting a collaborative environment:

Servant Leadership

Servant leaders focus on the needs of the team, fostering growth and development. They listen, understand, and support their team members, promoting a culture of collaboration and mutual respect.

Transformational Leadership

Transformational leaders motivate their teams by establishing a clear vision. They cultivate an environment of creativity and encourage input, pushing team members to work towards common goals.

Participative Leadership

Participative leaders value input from team members in decision-making. By encouraging collaboration, they foster ownership and a sense of belonging among their team.

Becoming an effective leader is not about exerting authority; it is about empowering others. By creating an environment that emphasizes empowerment, leaders set the stage for team members to thrive, innovate, and contribute meaningfully. At its core, leadership is about uplifting others and enabling them to realize their full potential. Investing in team members leads to a dynamic environment where everyone can succeed, ultimately resulting in collective achievements.

To create impactful change, embrace the core principles of empowering leadership. Recognize that your role is not to dictate but to facilitate trust, growth, and collaboration. The real power to lead lies in empowering others, making this the foundation of your leadership approach.

ARTICLE 16

Are You A Leader Of Good Character?

Effective leadership has become a hot topic in a world constantly in motion. Organizations seek leaders who not only possess skills but also showcase character. Why is character so important? A leader with good character inspires teams, builds trust, and creates a positive environment for all. So, what traits make up a leader of good character? Let's explore this vital subject.

Understanding Leadership Character

Character involves the moral and ethical values guiding a person's choices. When discussing leadership character, we're focusing on essential traits that shape how a leader connects with team members and the wider community. Leaders marked by strong character exhibit consistent values, integrity, and a true commitment to serving others.

For example, a survey conducted by the Harvard Business Review found that 67% of employees believe their leaders lack integrity. In contrast, 78% feel motivated when they trust their leaders. This illustrates the importance of character in fostering an effective work environment. A leader with sound character operates with authenticity. They act in a genuine manner that is deeply aligned with their values. This approach not only builds trust but strengthens connections within the team.

The Key Qualities of a Noble Leader

Integrity

Integrity is the bedrock of good character in any leader. It means being honest, consistent, and sticking to ethical principles. Leaders who show integrity earn their team's respect. They are willing to make hard choices and remain transparent about the implications. For instance, an Ethics & Compliance Initiative study highlighted that organizations with high-integrity leaders experience 25% higher employee engagement rates. When integrity is evident in leadership, it inspires the whole team to act similarly and creates a positive workplace culture.

Empathy

Empathy—understanding and relating to the feelings of others—is crucial for good leadership. Leaders who practice empathy forge stronger connections with their team members. They recognize that employees have lives outside of work and respect their challenges.

Consider this: Companies with empathetic leaders report up to 30% higher employee retention rates. By fostering an atmosphere of open communication and understanding, leaders build loyalty and encourage innovation within their teams.

Accountability

Good leaders take full responsibility for their actions and decisions. They recognize mistakes and learn from them—never playing the blame game. This accountability nurtures a culture of trust within the organization. Research shows that organizations with accountable leaders see a 20% increase in team cohesion. When leaders own their decisions, team members are more likely to do the same, leading to improved outcomes and enhanced communication.

Courage

Courage goes beyond facing challenges; it also means standing up for what is right. Courageous leaders make tough decisions and advocate for their team, even when it is not the popular choice. A recent survey found that teams led by courageous leaders are 35% more likely to feel confident in their roles. When leaders demonstrate bravery, it empowers employees to take risks and innovate.

Humility

While confidence is vital, humility rounds out the ideal leader. Humble leaders are approachable, listen actively, and recognize they do not have all the answers. They appreciate the strengths of their team members and welcome diverse viewpoints. According to a study by the Center for Creative Leadership, humble leaders foster 45% more effective teamwork. This humility creates an inclusive atmosphere where everyone feels valued, encouraging collaboration and fresh ideas.

Vision

A powerful vision drives great leaders and their teams toward common goals. Noble leaders clearly articulate a vision that aligns with their organization's values, inspiring others to pursue it. Sharing their vision motivates employees and instills a sense of purpose. Organizations guided by a clear vision often see a 50% increase in productivity as team members align their efforts towards shared objectives.

Reflecting on Your Leadership Character

Now that you know the essential traits that define a leader of good character, it's time to self-reflect. Consider the following questions:

1. Do you consistently exhibit integrity in your choices?
2. How often do you practice empathy in your interactions?
3. Are you willing to accept accountability for your actions?
4. Do you have the courage to stand up for what is right?

5. Are you humble enough to acknowledge others' contributions?

6. Do you have a clear vision that inspires those around you?

Evaluating your leadership character is a powerful step toward personal and professional development. Recognizing your strengths allows you to leverage them effectively while acknowledging areas needing improvement can lead to lasting change.

The Path Forward

Character plays a crucial role in effective leadership. Leading with integrity, empathy, accountability, courage, humility, and vision distinguishes noble leaders and sets a powerful example for others. As you take time for self-reflection and growth, remember that leadership means serving, inspiring, and uplifting others.

ARTICLE 17

Unleashing The Power Of Positive Thinking: A Leader's Secret to Success

Great leaders are distinguished by more than their decision-making abilities—they have the capacity to inspire those around them. One of the most influential tools at their disposal is the cultivation of a positive mindset. While positive thinking is frequently equated with mere optimism, its impact in the realm of leadership is profound and far-reaching.

A leader's attitude serves as a catalyst, generating a ripple effect that can shape the culture of their team, promote a productive and supportive work environment, and ultimately pave the way for sustained success. Leaders who actively embrace and embody positive thinking not only enhance their own performance but also have a significant uplifting influence on their colleagues and team members. This environment of positivity fosters creativity, resilience, and collaboration, which are essential components of a high-performing team. In this article, we will delve deeper into the myriad ways positive thinking can enhance leadership effectiveness.

We will discuss practical strategies for cultivating a positive mindset, such as mindfulness practices, focusing on strengths, and encouraging open communication. Additionally, we will explore actionable methods for leveraging this powerful tool to drive both individual and collective success within an organization, demonstrating how a leader's positive perspective can transform challenges into opportunities and inspire greatness in others.

The Impact of Positive Thinking on Leadership

Positive thinking significantly enhances a leader's effectiveness in various dimensions. Numerous studies indicate that leaders who embrace an optimistic viewpoint are approximately 30% more effective in handling challenges and promoting creativity within their teams.

This increased effectiveness stems from their ability to approach problems with a solution-oriented mindset, enabling them to see potential opportunities rather than obstacles. As a result, these leaders not only identify viable solutions more readily but also motivate their teams to adopt a similar positive outlook, fostering a culture of collaboration and innovative thinking. Moreover, cultivating a positive mindset contributes to resilience for both leaders and their teams. When faced with failures or setbacks, leaders who prioritize positivity are better equipped to bounce back and provide their teams with guidance and support during tough times. This resilience not only helps them to recover more quickly from challenges but also instills a sense of trust and stability within their teams, encouraging members to persevere despite difficulties.

Additionally, the environment fostered by a positive leader significantly influences team morale. Employees who feel appreciated, respected, and engaged in their work typically experience a remarkable increase in productivity—often reported as high as 25%. This boost in productivity can be attributed to the psychological safety created by a leader who embodies positivity and encouragement.

When team members observe their leader maintaining a hopeful and enthusiastic demeanor, they are more likely to mirror that attitude, leading to a motivated and cohesive workforce. Ultimately, a positive atmosphere enhances individual and team performance and contributes to a thriving organizational culture.

Cultivating a Positive Mindset

To embody positivity as a leader, intentional practice is essential. Here are practical strategies to develop this mindset:

Practice Gratitude

Fostering gratitude is a powerful way to boost positivity. Take a moment to appreciate the positives in your work and your team. Make it a daily habit to write down three things you are thankful for. This practice helps shift your focus from challenges to opportunities, which can significantly enhance your mindset.

Surround Yourself with Positive Influences

The people you engage with can significantly shape your mindset. Surround yourself with enthusiastic individuals who motivate you to grow. Invest time in relationships that energize you. These connections can help create an environment of encouragement, which is vital for maintaining a positive attitude.

Embrace Constructive Feedback

Viewing feedback positively is essential for growth. Consider constructive criticism as an opportunity, not a personal attack. Encourage open communication within your team. When team members feel heard and appreciated, it fosters a culture where positive thinking can thrive.

Set Positive Goals

Goal-setting provides direction and purpose. Framing these goals positively can increase motivation and encourage better outcomes. Instead of expressing what you want to avoid, focus on what you wish to achieve. For example, instead of saying, "I want to decrease mistakes," articulate it as "I want to improve our accuracy by 20% this quarter." This shift promotes an atmosphere of positivity and possibility.

The Ripple Effect of Positivity on Team Dynamics

A leader's positive outlook can ripple through the entire team. When leaders exhibit positivity, team members are likely to adopt similar attitudes.

Building a Positive Team Culture

When leaders display positive behaviors, they contribute to a supportive team culture. This culture encourages collaboration and innovation, allowing team members to share ideas without fear of judgment. Celebrate small wins as a team. Recognition of each achievement—no matter how small—creates momentum and improves morale, fostering a lasting positive environment.

Enhancing Employee Engagement

Leaders who express positivity can increase employee engagement. Inspired employees contribute more effectively and align closely with the organization's goals.

In a positive environment, team members actively engage in their work, leading to improved performance and productivity. Research shows that workplaces with high employee engagement can have 18% higher productivity rates.

Reframe Difficult Situations

It's easy to slip into negativity during tough times. Instead, practice reframing challenges as growth opportunities. Ask yourself, "What can I learn from this?" or "How can this situation lead to creative solutions?" This shift in thinking encourages a solution-oriented mindset.

Maintain Perspective

During tough times, maintaining a broader perspective is crucial. Understand that setbacks are part of the leadership journey. When you focus on the bigger picture, you can cultivate resilience and motivate your team to persevere. Promoting a culture of positivity means acknowledging problems while maintaining an optimistic outlook towards solutions.

Positive thinking is an essential skill for leaders; it goes beyond being a soft skill to become a strategic advantage that drives success and fosters a healthy team environment. By embracing positivity, leaders can improve their effectiveness and inspire those around them, creating significant benefits throughout the organization. As leaders, committing to a positive mindset transforms challenges into opportunities and lessons learned. While the path to success has obstacles, a positive mindset helps leaders guide their teams with resilience and purpose, achieving greatness together.

Harness the power of positive thinking. It equips leaders with the tools to excel personally while uplifting everyone around them. As you navigate your leadership journey, let positivity be your guiding principle, and watch its profound impact on your success.

ARTICLE 18

The Hidden Dangers Of Quiet Passion In Organizations

In the dynamic and often high-pressure landscape of modern workplaces, organizations frequently place a premium on the vigor and enthusiasm of passionate employees. These individuals serve as catalysts within their teams, igniting projects with their innovative ideas, energizing their colleagues with their motivated spirit, and propelling the organization forward through their unwavering commitment to excellence. However, there comes a time when this vibrant passion may begin to wane.

When the excitement that once marked these employees' contributions starts to fade, it can signal troubling underlying issues that may be festering within the organization. This decline may manifest as a noticeable loss of joy, creativity, and genuine drive among team members, raising concerns about overall morale and engagement.

Consequently, it becomes imperative for organizations to take a closer look at the factors contributing to this decline in enthusiasm. Whether it is due to burnout, a lack of recognition, insufficient resources, or a disconnect from the organization's mission, addressing these root causes is crucial. By doing so, organizations can not only re-engage their passionate team members but also foster a healthier, more inspiring work environment that nurtures creativity and innovation.

The Importance of Passion in the Workplace

Passion plays a vital role in creating a thriving workplace. It not only ignites creativity but also inspires innovation and enhances productivity. Research shows that passionately engaged employees can boost their performance levels by up to 20% compared to those who may feel less connected.

This deep engagement fosters stronger collaboration among team members, contributing to a more vibrant and supportive work environment. However, it's important to recognize that even the most passionate individuals can go through quiet phases that might be overlooked. When they begin to withdraw, it can be a sign of underlying challenges within the organization, and it's essential to approach these moments with understanding and compassion.

Recognizing the Signs of Quiet Passion

The initial signs of concern often become evident when dedicated employees begin to withdraw from conversations, respond less frequently, or seem disengaged during meetings. These subtle changes can easily go unnoticed, particularly in organizations that prioritize results over the well-being of their team members.

It's important for organizations to pay close attention to these developments. If an employee who once contributed enthusiastically starts to hold back, it's crucial to investigate what might be causing this shift. Regular surveys and heartfelt one-on-one conversations can provide valuable insights into employee satisfaction. In fact, organizations that implement consistent feedback practices often see a significant boost in employee morale—up to 15%. By fostering an environment where employees feel heard and valued, organizations can help support their well-being and commitment.

The Dangers of Ignoring the Silent Voices

It's important to recognize the impact of moving from passion to silence within a team. When dedicated team members feel overlooked or invisible, it can lead to disengagement that spreads throughout the group. Their quietness doesn't just affect them; it can unintentionally foster a culture of disinterest that touches everyone.

In environments where silence prevails, we run the risk of stifling innovation. When our most passionate voices go unheard, we lose out on the creative ideas and unique perspectives that are vital for progress. It's heartbreaking to think that organizations might fall behind their competitors who prioritize open communication and a culture of engagement. By valuing and listening to these enthusiastic individuals, we can cultivate an atmosphere where everyone feels seen, heard, and inspired to contribute.

Creating an Open Culture

To combat the risks linked to quiet passion, organizations must focus on fostering an open and inclusive culture. Leadership plays a key role in promoting dialogue and actively seeking feedback from all employees. When workers know their opinions are valued, they are more inclined to share ideas and concerns.

Offering anonymous surveys and hosting open forums can boost the confidence of quieter employees to express themselves. Moreover, regularly recognizing employee achievements can significantly contribute to this positive environment. Celebrating successes and providing constructive feedback cultivates an atmosphere where passion thrives.

Benefits of Engaging the Silent Passionate

Re-engaging quiet employees can produce remarkable outcomes. When these passionate individuals feel encouraged to share their thoughts, they can rejuvenate the organization. New perspectives often lead to innovative solutions and improvements that drive success. Additionally, involving them again can enhance overall morale, creating a workflow that benefits everyone. When employees feel their contributions are valued, it leads to better retention rates and a stronger organizational culture. Encouraging collaboration among passionate individuals promotes a lively exchange of ideas. This can lead to exciting projects and innovative approaches that challenge traditional thinking.

Strategies for Organizational Leaders

Leaders play a vital role in keeping passionate individuals engaged. Regular check-ins are essential to create open conversations about workloads, challenges, and growth opportunities.

- **Encourage Transparency:** Create a communication policy that promotes openness at all organizational levels.

- **Diversity of Communication Channels:** Recognize that different individuals may prefer various ways of expressing themselves. Provide multiple feedback channels—such as one-on-one meetings, group discussions, or digital platforms—so all voices can be heard.

• **Invest in Training:** Offering training focused on communication and teamwork enhances employees' ability to connect, building a supportive atmosphere.

• **Set Up Mentorship Programs:** Pairing passionate individuals with mentors can guide them back to active participation and foster a sense of belonging.

• **Promote Work-Life Balance:** Helping employees maintain a healthy work-life balance reduces burnout and keeps their passion alive. Organizations should prioritize mental health and well-being support.

Rediscovering the Power of Passion

When organizations recognize and cultivate the passions of their employees, they can transform quiet struggles into vibrant contributions. By identifying the signs of quiet passion and implementing effective strategies, companies can foster an environment where everyone feels comfortable sharing their thoughts. Encouraging a culture of open communication and celebrating employee contributions empowers passionate individuals and drives organizations toward greater innovation and success. As leaders, the responsibility lies with you to nurture the passions that fuel your organization. When passion is genuinely expressed, the entire organization has the potential to thrive.

ARTICLE 19

Recognizing Your Inherent Worth

In today's fast-paced and often competitive environment, it's all too easy to succumb to the habit of comparing ourselves to those around us. Social media, in particular, amplifies this tendency, presenting curated images of success and happiness that can distort our understanding of self-worth. As a result, we may find our self-esteem closely linked to external validation and how others perceive us. This dependency can lead to feelings of inadequacy and frustration, especially when it seems that we fall short of societal expectations or the accomplishments of our peers.

However, it is crucial to remember that your intrinsic value remains unchanged regardless of someone else's inability to recognize or appreciate it. Each person possesses unique qualities, strengths, and potential that contribute to their worth. This post aims to delve deeper into the idea of self-worth, offering insights into how you can better recognize and appreciate your inherent value.

We will explore the psychological impact of external opinions, highlighting how they can shape our self-perception and emotional well-being. By understanding these influences, we can begin to differentiate between our true selves and the distorted views formed by comparison. Additionally, numerous effective strategies can be implemented daily to help affirm and boost your self-worth. These might include practices such as self-reflection, positive affirmations, and surrounding yourself with supportive individuals who uplift you rather than diminish your sense of self.

Ultimately, cultivating a strong sense of self-worth is a journey that involves recognizing the beauty of your uniqueness and embracing your character, regardless of societal benchmarks. Remember, your value is inherent, not contingent on external acknowledgment.

The Nature of Self-Worth

Self-worth is an intrinsic quality that reflects how we view ourselves. It involves deep beliefs, perceptions, and attitudes about our own value. While it's common to be affected by factors like relationships and societal expectations, it's crucial to understand that others do not define your self-worth. For instance, professionals who receive negative feedback might find their confidence shaken. Yet, their skills, backed by experience and achievements, still hold value. Realizing that your worth stems from personal experiences, skills, and the unique qualities that define you is a vital step towards building a solid sense of self.

The Impact of Others' Perceptions

People's perceptions can significantly affect how we see ourselves. Whether due to their biases or personal insecurities, their inability to appreciate our value can lead to self-doubt. It's important to remember that their opinions are often reflections of their own struggles. For example, if a colleague fails to recognize your contributions in a group project, it may signal their own issues rather than a lack of quality in your work. Your skills as a team player or your innovative ideas still matter, regardless of others' viewpoints.

Understanding Your Unique Skills and Strengths

Identifying your core strengths is critical in building self-worth. Everyone brings something special to the table, whether empathy, creativity, analytical thinking, or resilience. To get started, keep a journal where you jot down big and small achievements.

For instance, if you've completed a challenging project or helped a friend through a tough time, write it down. This exercise shows you tangible proof of your capabilities and serves as a reminder of your value. Research shows that individuals who regularly practice self-reflection and acknowledge their achievements often report a 30% increase in their self-esteem.

Surround Yourself with Affirming Voices

Your environment plays a significant role in shaping your self-perception. Surrounding yourself with supportive people can profoundly impact how you view yourself. Seek relationships and communities that uplift you. For example, joining a local club focused on your interests can connect you with like-minded individuals who celebrate individual strengths. Being part of an encouraging atmosphere helps you recognize and affirm your inherent worth.

Celebrate Your Achievements

Recognizing and celebrating your achievements reinforces your self-worth. Every small milestone matters. For instance, if you've learned a new skill or helped a colleague solve a problem, give yourself credit. Taking time to reflect and reward yourself boosts your self-esteem and creates a positive cycle that continually affirms your value. Studies show that individuals who celebrate their accomplishments report a 25% higher satisfaction with life.

The Role of Self-Compassion

Enhancing your sense of worth is greatly aided by self-compassion. Life can be challenging, and treating yourself kindly during tough times is essential.

Instead of being your harshest critic, practice self-empathy. When faced with setbacks, acknowledge your feelings without judgment. This technique builds resilience and fosters a deeper connection to your worth during challenging moments.

Challenge Negative Thoughts

To affirm your value, it's vital to combat negative thoughts. When you find yourself struggling with self-doubt, question whether these beliefs stem from facts or external opinions. Transform negative thoughts into positive affirmations. For example, if you think, "I can't do this," reframe it to, "I am capable and learning." Practicing this strategy nurtures a healthier self-image and reinforces your inherent worth.

Mindfulness and Self-Awareness

Engaging in mindfulness can enhance your self-awareness and provide clarity. By focusing on the present, you can better understand your thoughts and feelings, separating your self-worth from external opinions. Incorporating practices like meditation or yoga into your daily routine can create a stronger connection with yourself. Even spending just a few minutes daily in mindful reflection can significantly boost your sense of personal worth.

Embracing Your True Value

Recognizing your inherent worth is a continuous journey that requires patience and effort. Remember that **your value does not decrease based on someone's inability to see your worth**.

By understanding what shapes your self-worth, surrounding yourself with positive influences, celebrating your unique strengths, and practicing self-compassion, you can cultivate a resilient sense of your value. Always hold onto the truth that your worth is an intrinsic quality that remains constant, independent of others' perceptions. By embracing this perspective, you can lead a life filled with confidence and authenticity, allowing your true self to shine.

ARTICLE 20

Leading With Respect

In today's rapidly changing world, leadership means more than just managing tasks or driving profits. One of the most important aspects of effective leadership is the ability to treat everyone with respect. Respect is a foundational element that drives collaboration, sparking innovation and creating a sense of belonging among team members.

Understanding Respect in Leadership

Respect is a multifaceted concept that encompasses the acknowledgment of the intrinsic worth of every individual, irrespective of their role, status, or background. In the context of leadership, respect entails not only appreciating the unique contributions each team member brings to the table but also actively engaging with their perspectives and insights. This means creating an environment where ideas can be freely exchanged and feedback is both constructive and encouraging.

When leaders demonstrate respect, they cultivate a workplace culture characterized by trust and transparency. In such an atmosphere, team members are more likely to feel safe and empowered to express their thoughts and opinions without fear of judgment or retribution. This idea illustrates that effective leadership goes beyond mere authority and direction; it emphasizes the importance of uplifting and enabling others to reach their full potential.

Research indicates a strong correlation between respect and employee engagement, with approximately 70% of workers reporting that their level of engagement significantly increases when they feel respected by their leaders and peers. This underscores the vital connection between a respectful workplace and the motivation to perform at one's best, ultimately contributing to higher productivity and job satisfaction. Recognizing and fostering respect within a team is essential for building a cohesive and driven workforce.

The Impact of Respect on Your Team

When team members feel genuinely respected, it can profoundly transform team dynamics and overall productivity. In environments where respect is deeply embedded in the culture, individuals come together with a sense of unity and belonging, which in turn fosters stronger collaboration and deeper understanding among peers.

This nurturing atmosphere encourages open communication and promotes a culture of mutual support. As a result, team members are more willing to share ideas and contribute, leading to enhanced creativity and more effective problem-solving strategies. Moreover, respect cultivates an inclusive environment where diverse perspectives are acknowledged and celebrated rather than merely tolerated. A compelling study conducted by McKinsey & Company has shown that organizations prioritizing gender and racial diversity are 35% more likely to outperform their industry counterparts in terms of financial success.

By recognizing and valuing individual differences within the team, organizations can leverage these unique perspectives to tap into their collective strengths, ultimately enriching the collaborative experience and driving innovation. Trust stands out as another essential component of effective leadership in this context. A leader who consistently demonstrates respect and appreciation for their team members lays a solid foundation for trustworthiness.

When employees feel that their opinions are valued and their contributions are recognized, this fosters a profound sense of loyalty to the organization and its objectives. Such loyalty can be transformative, encouraging team members to align their personal goals with the broader mission of the organization.

Also, fostering a culture of trust can significantly impact employee morale and motivation. Studies show that employees who are respected in their workplace often exceed expectations and go above and beyond for their teams. For instance, businesses prioritizing high employee engagement have reported profitability increases of up to 21%.

This statistic underscores the profound impact a culture rooted in respect and trust can have not just on individual performance but on overall organizational success and well-being within the team. By intentionally cultivating these values, organizations can create a thriving workplace where every member feels empowered and valued.

Leading by Example

A leader's actions play a critical role in shaping an organization's overall atmosphere and culture. When leaders consistently demonstrate respect in their interactions, they set a powerful example and create an environment where every team member feels valued and heard. For instance, leaders who engage in active listening—genuinely paying attention to the thoughts and concerns of their team members—foster an atmosphere of open communication. This practice can involve asking insightful questions, acknowledging contributions, and showing empathy toward challenges faced by individuals.

Moreover, providing timely and constructive feedback is essential for nurturing a culture of respect. When feedback is given in a thoughtful manner, it encourages continuous growth and reinforces the notion that every team member is important to the collective success. Recognizing and celebrating the achievements of others, whether through verbal praise, team shout-outs, or formal awards, further cultivates a sense of camaraderie and appreciation within the team.

This holistic approach to leadership does more than strengthen interpersonal bonds; it embeds respect into the organization's core values. When respect becomes a foundational element of the team's culture, it creates a safe and empowering space where everyone can thrive, collaborate effectively, and contribute to shared goals with enthusiasm and commitment. Ultimately, leaders who embody these principles not only enhance team dynamics but also drive the organization towards greater success.

Navigating Conflicts Respectfully

Conflicts will inevitably arise within any team. How leaders handle these conflicts can either strengthen or weaken mutual respect among team members. By addressing conflicts with an emphasis on respect, leaders can steer discussions toward finding common ground. This approach reduces tension and fosters resilience within the team, as members learn to handle disagreements while keeping shared goals in sight.

Practical Steps to Instill Respect in a Team

To nurture a culture of respect, leaders can adopt several practical strategies:

- **Active Listening:** Make a genuine effort to listen to team members without interruption. Even differing viewpoints should be validated, showing everyone's perspective is valued.

- **Acknowledgment:** Regularly highlight individual and team accomplishments, regardless of size. Recognition fosters a sense of belonging and importance.

- **Open Door Policy:** Encourage team members to approach you with concerns, feedback, or suggestions. This practice reinforces that their voices genuinely matter.

The impact of leading with respect extends beyond immediate interactions. Organizations that promote a respectful environment attract and retain top talent more effectively. Employees who feel valued are more engaged and committed to their work, leading to increased productivity.

Additionally, a respectful leadership culture enhances an organization's reputation. Companies known for treating employees and stakeholders well are often viewed positively by customers and potential recruits, significantly impacting business success.

CONCLUSION

Exceptional leadership's impact extends well beyond immediate business metrics and outcomes. Effective leaders play a crucial role in fostering employee engagement by creating environments where team members feel valued, empowered, and motivated to contribute their best efforts. They actively cultivate a strong organizational culture that aligns with the company's core values, ultimately leading to enhanced collaboration and a shared sense of purpose among employees.

Engaged employees are typically 17% more productive and 21% more profitable for their companies. Effective leaders take the time to understand their team members' strengths and aspirations, aligning individual goals with organizational objectives. For example, a leader might encourage a team member with an interest in graphic design to collaborate on marketing materials, which not only boosts morale but also engages that employee more deeply in their work. Outstanding leadership serves as a transformative force that not only influences day-to-day operations but also shapes the future trajectory of organizations. By acknowledging and investing in the multifaceted role of leadership, companies can ensure not just their immediate success but their long-term sustainability and impact in an ever-changing world.

ABOUT THE AUTHOR

Gifford Thomas is the founder of Leadership First and the author of the Amazon bestsellers **Unlock the Hidden Leader: Become the Leader You Were Destined to Be** and **The Inspirational Leader: Inspire Your Team to Believe in the Impossible.** With over 15 years of experience in leadership development, Gifford is passionate about empowering leaders to cultivate extraordinary organizations that inspire and motivate their people to achieve their fullest potential.

Gifford holds an MBA from Henley Business School, University of Reading and a B.A. in Business Management from Anglia Ruskin University. Leadership

First is a dynamic platform that inspires over 6.5 million leaders daily, sharing powerful leadership quotes and articles from the world's leading thought leaders. As a member of the Harvard Business Review Advisory Council, a council member with GLG, and an advisor for visasQ Inc., Gifford is deeply committed to empowering leaders to navigate the challenges of today's competitive landscape while helping leaders become the very best version of themselves.